colin cowie
chic

colin cowie chic

the guide to life as it should be

Clarkson Potter/Publishers
New York

Copyright © 2007 by CAW Cowie, Inc.,
a California Corporation

Published in the United States by
CLARKSON POTTER/PUBLISHERS,
an imprint of the Crown Publishing Group, a division of
RANDOM HOUSE, INC., NEW YORK.
www.crownpublishiing.com
www.clarksonpotter.com

Clarkson N. Potter is a trademark and Potter and colophon are
registered trademarks of Random House, Inc.

Library of Congress Cataloging-in-Publication Data
Cowie, Colin, 1962–
Colin Cowie chic: the guide to life as it should be / Colin
Cowie. — 1st ed.
p.   cm.
Includes index.
1. House furnishings.   2. Entertaining.
3. Interior decoration.   4. Office decoration.
5. Travel paraphernalia.   6. Travel etiquette.   7. Life skills.
I. Title.   II. Title: Colin Cowie Chic.
III. Title: Guide to life as it should be.
TX311.C69   2007
645—dc22   2007006080

ISBN 978-0-307-34179-2

Photography and illustration
credits appear on page 272.

Printed in China

DESIGN BY JENNIFER K. BEAL

10   9   8   7   6   5   4   3   2   1

First Edition

This book is
d e d i c a t e d
to all the people who have contributed to my philosophy on style and have helped shape my life. I owe my deepest gratitude to: Oprah Winfrey, Pamela Fiori, Martha Nelson, Margo Baker-Barbakow, Stuart Brownstein, Charles Allem, Murat Atabarut, Frank Bowling, Jonathan Beare, Sloan and Roger Barnett, and of course my parents, Gloria and the late Cecil Cowie.

contents

introduction

Have you ever left a party and thought, *Wow, they really know how to do it right?* Have you ever felt so welcome as a weekend houseguest that you couldn't wait to return? Have you ever received a bouquet of flowers, for no reason other than that the sender remembered you love Schiaparelli-pink peonies? Have you ever gotten a thank-you note that you've wanted to save forever? Have you ever been served a cocktail so enticing you wanted a refill after taking your first sip? I feel so lucky to have had these experiences, and it's one of my greatest pleasures to make people feel the same way when they spend time with me.

Whether stopping by for a snappy cocktail or hanging out for a long, lazy weekend, everyone who comes into my home is treated like royalty. I take enormous pride in my lifestyle, and I'm thrilled when my clients say that they wish they could live the way I do—as though there's some big secret to living well. I don't have nearly the wealth they have, or the staff most of them employ, or a home the size of most of theirs, but one thing I do have is a passion for enjoying life, twenty-four hours a day, seven days a week, at 120 miles per hour (100 just isn't fast enough!). My not-so-secret secrets? An abundance of style, with clever organizational techniques and ruthless editing thrown in for good measure.

How do you define style? It's not about the brand of watch on your wrist, the pricey designer outfit you're wearing, or a fancy zip code. Style starts with self-respect, which leads to the respect you give to, and get from, other people. Whether I'm at home, in the office, or traveling, I always go that extra mile to treat myself and the people around me with the same amount of generosity, courtesy, and mindfulness that I'd like to receive from them. I live by this principle! Style is all about being conscious: of yourself, of your surroundings, and especially of the people in your life, both friends and strangers.

Colin Cowie Chic is a guide to gracious living in a very real, practical sense, regardless of budget. It doesn't matter if you live alone and do all the cooking and cleaning yourself or have a houseful of staff attending to your every whim. Living a full life starts with knowing the basics. Once you have that blueprint for elegant style and excellent manners, you can begin building on your vision—and from there, the sky's the limit!

Think of your life as you would a bank account; you can't constantly make withdrawals without making a few deposits. Whether you need a chilled pomegranate martini at the end of the day, a relaxing bath by candlelight while listening to a great piece of music, a quiet hour of meditation, or a bike ride for an hour in the morning followed by a balanced, healthy breakfast, it's important to replenish yourself with a shot of pure, unadulterated pleasure. It's not about treating yourself well every now and then; it's about living a lifestyle that nourishes you every day. Slipping your tired feet into a pair of cushy slippers (preferably cashmere), savoring a shower with your favorite soaps and scrubs, or escaping into a wonderful book while savoring a well-rounded glass of Bordeaux aren't indulgences—in today's frenetic world, they're necessities.

We all deserve to live a rich life, and **Colin Cowie Chic** will guide the way. I want you to go out (or stay in!) confident in the knowledge that you're at the top of your game. I want you to get the best table in the restaurant, the upgrade to the finest suite, the invitation to the party you've been aching to attend. And once you're at that party, I want you to know what to say and how to say it! Even if you only embrace a few of my tips, ideas, shortcuts, and inspirations, you'll discover that there really is no mystery to making the most of every moment. This book will put you in the fast lane to achieving your best life with minimal stress and a major payoff.

We cover everything from **how to receive guests to how to make a bed, tip the waiter, avoid jet lag, navigate the uncharted territory of e-mail etiquette, earn accolades at**

the office, and even lay out a lavish buffet. I've included the everyday basics and niceties that have put me in good stead while dealing with everyone from New York cabdrivers to Middle Eastern royalty. **Colin Cowie Chic** isn't a prim, dusty manual for your great-grandparents' generation (you'll find no footmen or finger bowls!); **it's an essential bible to how we can live a passionate and rewarding life right now.** In it, I share what I do on a daily basis, and what I've learned over the course of a lifetime from all my travels and from the people who've taught me the most: my parents. My mother, Gloria Cowie, instilled in me one of the most vital lessons in the world: that large gestures and small touches—niceties combined with a serious dash of chic and style—*do* make a big difference. And my late father, Cecil Cowie, a true bon vivant, showed me that with creativity, generosity, and that extra 20 percent of pure passion, we're all capable of transforming the average into the extraordinary, the mundane into the magical, and the time we have on this planet into a remarkable ride.

Here's hoping that you have fun and live every day to its absolute fullest.

grace, flair, poise (aka personal style): where do I find it and how do I get it?

It's one of the questions people ask me most often: What is personal style? All of us think we know it when we see it. It's the woman in the corner of the room, looking cool in her palazzo pants, easy blouse, and subtly billowing scarf. It's the man in the black cashmere sweater, blazer flung with seeming haphazardness over one shoulder. Looking at them, you might think that style has something to do with a drop-dead wardrobe, a fantastic watch, a killer pair of shoes, a sleek haircut, a legendary zip code: in short, a bank account fat enough to re-create the look and the life of a movie star.

But to me, great personal style is less about what (and how much) you buy and what you wear (and how much it costs) than it is about self-esteem and self-respect, which invariably invite respect from others. Great style is a reflection of how you feel about yourself, whether you're getting dressed in the morning, grooming yourself, creating a stylish home, traveling abroad, or earning the respect of your colleagues at work. It's the kitchen that's loaded with personality, the über-inviting dining room, the guest bedroom so lush and welcoming you feel like extending your stay a year!

Yes, I can completely understand why people today are confused about what style really means. We live in a world where we've advanced further technologically than we have socially. It's easy to be unsure about how we should behave in public and in private. How, for example, do we walk into a room and make a lasting and confident first impression? How should we wear our hair? What cut of suit works best on us? How should we treat other people? How do we welcome guests into our home? How do we set the table or write a heartfelt note?

The important thing to always remember is *to care.* And always think "elegant," so you look and act your absolute 100 percent best, every day of your life.

You Have Only One Chance to Make a First Impression

Life, I've always thought, is like theater. The lights dim . . . the crowd hushes . . . the curtain goes up . . . and the first five minutes clue you in as to whether you're going to enjoy the rest of the show . . . or begin furtively eyeing the exit signs. It's the same way with people. Our initial impression of a new acquaintance is indelible! When we first encounter a stranger, curiosity, chemistry, and interest are created and engaged — or not! When you're meeting someone for the first time, stand up straight, keep your shoulders back and your head held high. Greet people while looking in their eyes, with the warmest smile you can muster! No one will forget you.

"At the very least, women should always wear mascara, lipstick, and some blush. Men, too, should be well-groomed: hair cut, shirt pressed."

one

a gracious home: public spaces

Well, Come Inside

Your home is not only where you live; it's also your sanctuary. And it doesn't matter what or where you call home. It could be a studio apartment, a newlywed couple's starter house, an antique-laden 1700s Colonial, or a gleaming mountain-top eagle's nest filled with all the snazziest stainless-steel gadgets. Size and budget don't matter. What counts—what's indispensable—is making the space where you live relaxing and inviting, as well as a true reflection of who you are. As Americans, unfortunately, we have mastered the art of *appearances*: We've created beautiful houses and apartments, and collected many things over the years, but most of us don't really *live* in our homes. From the mansions of Beverly Hills to the lofts and town houses of Manhattan to all places inbetween, I can't count the number of residences I've walked into that have no essence of real life or welcoming energy, no feeling of who lives there, no sense of joy or communion. Very often they're flat, lifeless, picture-perfect shells to be admired rather than lived in and savored. For me, that's completely missing the point. We all deserve to live well and live our very best life possible.

My home is my refuge, my playground, my base of operations, my pride and joy. I use my living room sofa, my dining room table, my very best china, my crystal stemware, and every single one of my favorite things as often as possible—and I do so with pleasure and gratitude that they're mine. The people who created the beautiful objects we have in our

homes did so in order for us to enjoy them (just think of the stories vintage silver would tell if it could!). No matter if you live in a cramped one-room studio, or if your house resembles the Petit Trianon at Versailles, the most important element in any home is its welcoming spirit.

It's All About You!

How you live, how you treat yourself, how you take care of your things, and how you roll out the red carpet for your guests—these four elements are the most accurate barometers of personal style. Today we have more opportunities to show great taste than we've ever had before, and quality, well-designed products are available at every price point, in stores ranging from Bloomingdale's to Wal-Mart. Leaf through a home-design magazine for inspiration. They're full of resources, recommended Web sites, tips, ideas, and strategies for a life filled with beauty, passion, romance, and order. You can easily and quickly turn any space into a home with a bit of imagination, a new coat of paint, a set of slipcovers, a flowering plant, or a few fabulous flea-market finds. Permission granted to use your imagination, and instincts, to create a home that is utterly you.

Decorating a Home

It's important that you understand how you're going to live in your home. Regardless of what you design, it's crucial to see the big picture in your mind's eye. Who are you (or who do you want to be)? What kind of lifestyle do you lead? What's the general feeling you'd like to convey in your kitchen, your living room, your dining room? Gather magazine clippings, visit Web sites, and go online to create a dossier of tear sheets that best help you describe and articulate your vision. What you like and what you don't like are of equal importance.

Having said that, the most important goal of decorating is to feel comfortable in your own home. It's your personal space, not a stage set! Still puzzled? Regardless of the size of your place, you can hire a professional to assist you, guide you, or direct you. If you don't have the budget for outside help, don't worry. Many people give their homes great style without breaking the bank. Whether you're contemporary and minimalist or more the country-cottage type, you'll be able to fill in the details around your lifestyle, be it casual or formal, by knowing the big picture. Here are a few pointers:

1. Decide on a color palette. What is the principal color and what are the accent colors? Is there one color scheme or two? For example, many people choose to use color to differentiate the living and entertaining areas from the sleeping areas. Collect paint samples and paint chips to test on your walls before making a final decision. How a color looks on a paint chip and how it looks on your walls are two different things.

2. Create the shell—that is, the walls and floors—first, followed by the ceilings, doors, and windows. Select fabrics, textures, and finishes that suit the space and your tastes.

3. Dress up fireplaces and windowsills with molding, artwork, and colorful touches.

4. Work from a floor plan. Install the largest pieces of furniture first, then fill in the spaces around them with smaller pieces. A carpet, drapes, shades and blinds, and finally your accessories: framed pictures, gorgeous bowls, decorative pieces.

5. Celebrate and bring your home to life by adding foliage, flowers, candles, music, drinks, and your favorite colorful people.

Order in the House

The foundation of any well-run home is cleanliness and order. An orderly house will not only give you pleasure, it will also make everything in your life, from writing a thank-you note the day after a fabulous evening to opening your home to overnight guests, that much more effortless. Living elegantly means creating a place you look forward to coming home to, a place where you can entertain happily, harmoniously, generously—and without hassles or headaches.

I may be juggling thirty different crises at once (and usually am), but if my home is tidy and in order, I feel as though my *life* is in order and I can take on anything. I love walking into an intelligently designed, immaculate kitchen. I love opening the freezer door and finding everything I need neatly stacked: frozen appetizers ready to be popped into the oven, decorative ice cubes available to enliven a chic cocktail, chicken stock waiting to form the base of a delicious homemade soup. In the closet, I love finding my shirts arranged from light to dark, short-sleeve to long, beautifully starched, and hanging from matching hangers. I love clean, polished surfaces that are stripped of any unnecessary clutter. I love opening my desk drawers and immediately finding business cards, personal stationery, pens, and my cell phone charger. And at night, I love retiring to a bedroom so pulled together and luxuriously welcoming that I could easily mistake it for a five-star hotel suite.

A home filled with knickknacks and collectibles stacked and sprawled on every free surface may give visitors the feeling that you're holding a spur-of-the-moment garage sale. Keep the things that are precious to you close by and available so they can be used on a regular basis. Everything else should be stored in a safe place, not left out on display. Serving bowls should be on the tables only when they're overflowing with food, and there's nothing at all exciting about an empty vase perched on a windowsill (even if it's Lalique!). Less is definitely more! For example, a simple vase with one exotic flower on a central table can be more astonishing than that same vignette surrounded by fourteen framed pictures and half a dozen *objets* from your last European vacation.

"Knowing how to organize your home for living is the foundation for living with true style."

Instead, keep a separate closet or cupboard where you can store your collection of decorative items. When you bring them out for entertaining, they'll seem brand-new again. Use your pieces to create varied and interesting vignettes and fresh atmospheres, then put them away for the next time the mood strikes. Invest in drawer dividers, baskets, and closet organizers. Trays and decorative bowls can also be fantastic containers for odds and ends such as keys and loose change. Create areas for everything you use, which will allow you to find what you're looking for when you're looking for it.

Try to take twenty minutes each day to tidy up and put things back where they belong. When you're having a few friends over for drinks or throwing a party, you shouldn't have to do a major all-day cleaning. The longer you delay straightening up, the more burdensome it is to clean, and your house will begin to look like Times Square after the ball drops on New Year's Eve. It's much better, and a lot less overwhelming, to maintain order and cleanliness as you move through your day. Granted, most people work and have to scramble to keep up with household chores. But ideally, you'll get to a point where with a bit of soap and water, a mop and a broom, some dimmer switches on the lights and a little music, your home should be ready to receive guests at practically a moment's notice. If possible, consider hiring someone to help you maintain order, such as a maid who comes in on a weekly basis. Otherwise, a little at a time goes a long way.

Home Basics: The Swiss-Watch Effect

Turning your house into your own personal sanctuary demands a little prep work. Think of your home as a Swiss watch, a sum of all its expertly working parts. Start with the function of each room. Make sure that everything you need is in place, then add the things you love. Remember that a well-organized home is always prepared, whether you're celebrating a wonderful occasion, waiting out a storm, or embarking on a leave-no-cabinet-unturned spring-cleaning. Here are some guidelines:

In General

- Sit down and format a fail-safe system for paying bills, maintaining your home's infrastructure, and cleaning in general. Mark these chores in your calendar so that you can carry them out regularly and in a timely way. I promise you will breathe easier, and your home will function more efficiently. Example: Create a time to clear your mail, and separate the bills and catalogs from the personal mail (place your bills in a file in a dedicated drawer). Each Sunday evening I go through the bills and make to-do lists for home and office. It prepares my mind and motivates me for the coming week.

- The most important thing at all times is to do upkeep on your home! Do whatever it takes so that if a guest moves a chair to the left, he won't find a mini-Pompeii of dust and ashes underneath. As far as my home is concerned, there's no such thing as *too* clean!

- Consider hiring a cleaning service, or an individual, to carry out a major furniture-moving, window-washing, carpet-cleaning, grease-eradicating, top-to-bottom housecleaning. Naturally, this will depend on where you live and whether or not you have children. If you live in a sunny climate, your windows will sparkle with a once-a-year cleaning. If you live by a storm-battered ocean, it's another story entirely! And if you have children, resign yourself to the fact that you will be tidying up constantly.

- If you cook regularly, make sure you clean the ventilators above the stove monthly (this reduces buildup and the risk of fire).

- Just as you never know when you'll want to throw a party, you never know when you'll be faced with an emergency. We live in a world of natural and unnatural disasters, from hurricanes and floods and earthquakes to unexpected power outages. (See my SOS sidebar on page 67 for tips on what to keep in an emergency supply closet.)

Always in Season

- In the spring and fall, you might need to install or remove window air conditioners, or replace storm windows with screens, or vice versa. By keeping the systems that run your home operating at high efficiency, including heating and air conditioning systems, the tasks that seem monumental won't feel like impossible dreams. Again, mark them in your calendar to remind yourself.

- At the start of every season, devote a weekend morning to storing last season's bedding and clothing (I prefer Sundays for these chores). Plastic containers or large plastic zipper bags will allow you to pack everything on an out-of-the-way shelf in the garage or attic, or under the bed. After all, it's no fun freezing in the winter or simmering in the summer! Add naphthalene balls or cedar chips to protect your out-of-season treasures from hungry critters.

- If you haven't already, clean and edit your clothing closets (see my tips on pages 55–59).

- Stock up! By keeping your home overflowing with basic staples and produce, beverages such as liquor, mineral water, soft drinks, Champagne and white wine on ice, you'll be prepared for the next cause for celebration or — *my* favorite kind of celebration — no reason at all! (See pages 38–46 for fridge, freezer, kitchen cabinet, and liquor essentials.)

- Make sure you don't forget to change the batteries in your smoke detectors, transistor radio, and emergency kit. I do it once a year, at the change to daylight savings.

"The key to great style is *ruthless* editing."

Minimum Daily Requirements

- Keep a calendar of household duties and responsibilities. Set aside time to do the handyman repairs, or else call someone in to replace missing lightbulbs, change locks, fix a loose hinge on a cabinet, or touch up paint. Create a file on your desktop with a list of to-dos around the house. Once there are four or five items stacked up, it's time to call in the handyman. Don't let your home fall into disrepair. You won't want to be there, and neither will your friends!

- To keep your home clean and sparkling, have the right cleaning products close at hand. Keep them readily accessible and all in one place, but safely out of reach from children and pets. Hint: Keep a roll of paper towels, glass cleaner, and all-purpose cleaner under the vanity in the bathroom for quick and easy cleanups.

- Save time by taking advantage of various services that deliver: liquor stores, grocery chains, and dry cleaners.

- Buy in bulk to save time and money.

Making the Connection: The Living Room

I like to think of the living room as the place where we can connect with our friends and family. I make sure that guests feel not only welcome there but also at home. *Mi casa es su casa!*

If life is theater, then my living room is one place where I can set the stage daily, weekly, monthly, or seasonally. To receive guests easily and comfortably:

- A living room should ideally have one—and sometimes two—conversation areas, with the focal point being a coffee table or a fireplace. This tends to concentrate the conversation (and also makes it more fun and intimate).

- On my coffee table, I might display a pile of books I enjoy; or a grouping of dazzling crystal candles around a low

vase packed abundantly with flowers; or a tall, thin vase with a single bloom or tropical leaf. The point is to create harmony by choosing among three or four elements, such as books, candles, and a floral or decorative objet d'art.

Whatever mood I choose, it's always set when my guests arrive. By lighting candles, I can add instant ambience for everyone and everything surrounding my coffee table. And I make sure there is still sufficient space all around to place glasses, an ice bucket, and a tray of hors d'oeuvres.

• I recommend that you keep personal photographs all in one place—atop the piano or a chest of drawers—but not on every single flat surface. Yes, the sight of photographs scattered everywhere can be homey and welcoming, but it can easily get out of hand. I place all my personal photos in my bedroom, library, or den.

colin cowie chic

Style Is Living in the Moment:
Respect Yourself

I avoid using paper napkins or paper plates, and not only for environmental reasons. Setting the table with a "real" plate, a cloth napkin, and appropriate flatware has become a way of life for me. I use my good things in both the kitchen and the dining room. This wasn't always the case. In 1994 the California Northridge earthquake shook me out of bed and broke many fine pieces I had collected over the years. Most pieces were vintage collectibles I'd hardly ever used. That's when I decided not to save my good things for another day. I now use my favorite things every day and get great joy from them every time I do! I make a very conscious attempt to surround myself with my most beautiful and special objects whenever and wherever possible. I have kept that promise, and would rather replace the chipped, broken, and fragile pieces than not use them at all.

In retrospect, it seems my self-esteem was telling me that, somehow, I wasn't deserving enough to use special things every day, that I should save them only for special occasions.

My suggestion: As often as possible, try to set the table for every meal, every single morning, noon, and night! Rather than eating on the run, or wolfing down a sandwich or a muffin over the kitchen sink, make a point of sitting down, setting the time aside to truly enjoy your meal even if you are on your own. Bring out washable napkins, place mats, a decorative bowl, and a drinking glass. No matter what I'm eating, whether it's scrambled eggs, take-out Chinese food, or a delicious rack of spring lamb with a side of crunchy potatoes, I take time to enjoy the ritual of dining, and I pay respect to myself each time I do. Take a meal and turn it into a moment!

Granted, this is somewhat less practical for those people who sleep through the alarm clock in the morning, torpedo head-first into the shower, scramble to get to work on time, race through a sandwich in fifteen minutes at their desks in order to make a one o'clock meeting, then speed home to face last night's leftovers. If you are stressed out and time-starved (and who isn't these days?), take the time at least once a week, and again during the weekend, to set a table, light candles, surround yourself with your best plates and glasses, and savor the blessings of how it could be. *Now* is all we have: Fill it to the brim whenever possible and appeal to all the senses when telling the story.

Eat, Drink, Love:
A Beautiful Dining Room

When I think about the different rooms in my home, a word immediately comes to mind for each. For the dining room, it's *share,* because it's always been the place where I share my most magical moments with friends and family. The living room has always been a place we *connect* with one another, and have conversation and cocktails.

Unfortunately, the dining room has largely been consigned to life's grand and sometimes stuffy occasions: Christmas Eve dinner, Easter lunch, and once-a-year family reunions. My theory is that most people avoid their dining rooms because they assume it will take too much time and hard work to create a welcoming environment with the kind of meal that befits the room's daunting reputation. But that's yesterday's thinking!

First, make a conscious decision to divorce your dining room from its associations with formality, and think of it as a place to share great times with company. Some of my most memorable moments were spent around the table in my family's dining room, laughing and telling stories with my parents, my siblings, and my friends. My mother always took the time to set the table, light a candle, and open a good bottle of wine. Thinking back, I can honestly say there is no substitute in the world for that great, cozy feeling, that sense of sharing and cohesion. We owe it to ourselves to take the time to enjoy these moments.

My dining room is ready for entertaining at a moment's notice. At a minimum, I adorn the table with a sculpture, and sometimes with a series of geometric vases. I also love using an abundance of unscented candles in the that room. Being a self-confessed ambience junkie, I can honestly say there is no more flattering light than candlelight.

Mirrors also bring instant glamour to a dining room. Hang them on the walls behind guests so that people are able to see themselves and one another. For a more formal approach, place them on the walls at either end of a banquet

table to create an enchanted look of infinity. Who doesn't love to see themselves bathed in candlelight?

If you have multiple lighting opportunities like ceiling lights, or art lights above paintings, or wall washers, keep them on separate dimmer switches so you can adjust the light and orchestrate the mood accordingly.

Finally, music is always a vital element in the dining room. It keeps the energy going and sets the tone for the night. Keep a selection of dinner-friendly playlists in your iPod, from light classical and jazz to contemporary compilations.

For much more information on entertaining at home, see chapter 4.

Food for Thought and Talk: The Kitchen

The trend toward a more casual lifestyle has transformed the kitchen from a place of unwashed dishes and meals on the run into the heart, soul, and red-hot center of our day-to-day lives. It is by far the busiest room in the house, and also the room where most of us seem to spend the greatest amount of time. The kitchen is the place where we can express the very best of who we are—and our style of entertaining—so keep it sexy and inviting. It's the extra dash of rum in the cocktail, a dose of love in the lasagna, and a spritz of extra starch in the napkin.

Whether I'm cooking, enjoying delicious meals, having heart-to-heart conversations with friends or family, arranging flowers for the house, or reading the *New York Post,* my kitchen is where a lot of my life takes place—and that includes dining.

(For more on what makes my kitchen run, see the photographs in the Home Gallery, pages 108 to 111.)

A Kitchen That Cooks

My kitchen is ideally laid out, as a living kitchen. I have a long table that seats eight to ten guests; I have top-notch Electrolux ICON appliances all within arm's reach, and the entire color palette is gray and white, which turns any color I bring into the kitchen into the main event, whether in the form of food, flowers, linens, or all of the above. At all times I display a couple of large tropical leaves in a bold vase or a flowering orchid and a trio of decorative candles, and I've installed dimmer switches galore and a killer sound system. These are the ingredients you need for creating an unforgettable ambience.

If I'm hosting fewer than ten guests, which is the number of seats my kitchen table can hold, I first serve cocktails by candlelight in the living room. Afterward, the group makes its way to the kitchen, which is when the *real* party gets under way. I sometimes set a stunning table for a seated dinner, or a buffet on the countertop, or very often I'll serve a meal family style on big platters in the middle of the table. However I choose to serve the food, I make sure it's inviting and abundant. If only my table could talk!!!

Even if your kitchen isn't state-of-the-art, or if you're working out of a much smaller space with a limited budget, there's still a multitude of ways to transform your kitchen from blah to breathtaking. If you don't have a great sound system already installed, take advantage of today's portable iPod speakers, which come in all shapes, sizes, and price ranges (or if you prefer CDs, a boombox will work nicely). Paint one kitchen wall a fun, wild color — or scour your local department stores for some chic, retro 1960s wallpaper. Find a vintage poster that reeks of personality, frame it, and place it center-stage! If you have a table in your kitchen, consider dressing it in some fabulous fabric patterns to create a one-of-a-kind tablecloth. Finally, scour flea markets for mismatched china and stemware — and set the table with various pieces, short and tall, wide and svelte (each one tells a story).

Nearly a decade ago, in my previous apartment on the Upper East Side of Manhattan, I decided on a whim to give my kitchen a major drab-to-fab makeover. I painted the whole room a rich ruby red, installed some speakers, put a few bold Turkish rugs on the floor, hung a vintage champagne poster, and made tablecloths for my stainless-steel worktable. I immediately started having dinner parties in the kitchen and cannot begin to tell you how much fun we had drinking bottles of wine, experimenting with new recipes, and laughing— a lot. It truly transformed the kitchen into the center of my existence.

Here are a few suggestions for a drab-to-fab kitchen makeover:

- Choose a color scheme with personality. Paint is the least expensive way to transform a space immediately and dramatically. For added drama, try painting stripes on a wall, or use a stencil and add a graphic pattern.

- Install dimmer switches on every light. Everybody, and I mean *everybody,* looks a million times better under mood-enhanced lighting. If harsh bulbs are installed overhead, and dimmer lights won't work, consider investing in some skin-tone-friendly fluorescent bulbs or purchasing some lighting gels in soft, face-flattering colors, such as blush pink or amber. Add multiple layers to get a more moody color.

- Add instant glamour to your kitchen with an assortment of candles, including votives, pillars, tapers, and a good fragrant candle. Light a few or a lot, and your kitchen will read as warm and inviting.

- A large tropical leaf, a potted flowering plant, or a bowl of green apples brings life to the space.

- Dress your kitchen table with fabric napkins, place mats, or table runners. I use fabric napkins for both my guests and for my everyday meals. Fabric napkins are inexpensive today, nicer to use, and most of all, you're doing the environment a favor by avoiding disposables that add to the world's overcrowded landfills. Many of them don't even require ironing!

As you transform your kitchen, keep in mind that your own sense of style will come from mixing and matching pieces to create a truly personal look. Unless you're a strict

"When designing, I always try to create a JDM (Jaw-Dropping Moment)."

minimalist, or live in a country-style or traditional home, personal style is more about *mixing* than it is about *matching*. What appeals to each of us visually is the engine that drives and creates our own sense of style. Don't worry about blending together two completely different styles of art. As long as the effect is beautiful and harmonious, the sky's the limit.

Cooking in Color

As you transform your kitchen into the heart of your home, here are a few color pointers:

- For a warm, sexy, sultry mood, use a passionate deep red paint.

- If you're after a more retro, youthful look, chocolate brown is always a warm and sexy option. Use this with white cabinets for a more updated look. My favorite Pantone colors are very good neutrals: shades of gray or light brown, mixed with parchment and bronze finishes. Add or subtract drapes, carpet or rugs, and lampshades to your heart's content!

- Whites and light grays say clean, modern, contemporary. They work spectacularly well with cool stone or wood surfaces and countertops.

- Use caramel or ecru for a relaxing country feeling, yellow for an unforgettable Provençal look, and bright green for pure joy.

- If you have young children, an unleashed bohemian spirit, or both, consider painting a side wall with blackboard paint. When you're not graffitiing your own murals, you can use it for recipes, grocery lists, and telephone numbers.

Talking Kitchens

Even if you don't consider yourself a great cook, here are a few basic principles to help you stock your kitchen:

- Place your everyday china, dishwater-proof glasses, and silverware in a cabinet near the kitchen table. Easy access is half the battle!

- Set aside a drawer to hold two styles of everyday place mats, runners, and complementary cloth napkins.

- Keep a collection of unscented votives, pillar candles, and a lighter within reach so you can add instant ambience, making even the simplest meal a dining experience.

- For easy entertaining, have a selection of beverages accessible, storing your wine bottles horizontally in a cool, dark area. A designated shelf or cabinet works well (see Cocktail Party Basics on page 141). The best option for wine storage (short of the dream item, a wine cellar!) is a home wine cooler.

- Keep your serving pieces on one shelf, and your cookware and mixing and measuring bowls all together in another place. Store kitchen appliances that you don't use every day—your slow cooker, cappuccino maker, turkey roaster, or fish poacher—in higher, more out-of-the-way cabinets. Don't tuck them away in the attic or garage where you'll never use them! And don't forget to recycle the boxes they came in!

- Keep a notepad with a pen and pencil next to the phone so you can jot down items you need to replenish, as well as phone calls that come in while you're cooking.

- If there's room, keep your cookbooks on a shelf in the kitchen; again, easy access is key, and this way, inspiration will be right at your fingertips.

- Arrange your spices alphabetically; otherwise, hunting down the bottle of cumin can be a nightmare. Tiered spice racks work best, because they'll allow you to identify spices and herbs easily.

The Well-Stocked Kitchen

Here's an easy guide to a well-appointed kitchen equipped to entertain any size group, from one to a hundred and one — every day, twice a week, or four times a year.

Cookware

I know full well that my kitchen is as well stocked as the best restaurant in town, and not everyone needs quite as much gear! That's exactly why I've divided the following list into Essentials; Nice to Have; and For the Gourmet-Inclined.

Essentials
- Large saucepan
- Medium saucepan
- Small saucepan
- Large skillet
- Small skillet
- Nonstick skillet
- Sauté pan
- Stockpot
- Colander
- Pasta pot
- Oven mitts

Nice to Have
- Vegetable steamer
- Sauté pans (large and small)

For the Gourmet-Inclined
- Wok
- Roasting pan
- Griddle
- Grill pan
- Double boiler

Cookware Materials: What You Need to Know

Quality Control—Pots and pans are not created equal! Always be on the lookout for thickness—also known as gauge—of material, as well as solid construction, such as riveted handles. Cheap cookware usually has to be replaced every year. Sturdy, well-made pots and pans can last a decade or longer with proper care.

Aluminum—Heats quickly and evenly, and with a nonstick surface inside, it is easy to clean.

Cast Iron—Absorbs and distributes heat evenly, and works best for frying, searing, browning, stewing, and baking

Copper—The oldest cookware metal and the most efficient conductor of heat, it is always lined with silver, tin, stainless steel, or a nonstick finish to avoid chemical reactions that discolor food.

Glass—Wonderfully versatile, it goes from oven to freezer to table to dishwasher, and into the microwave as well. It's easy to maintain, and you can often buy it in storable sets.

Stainless Steel—Extremely durable, it won't dent, stain, or scratch, and is often bonded with copper or aluminum to enhance heat conduction.

Cutlery and Flatware

Essentials
- A dozen five-piece place settings (butter knife, dinner knife, dinner fork, salad fork, and soup spoon) or use two different styles with six five-piece place settings each
- A dozen steak knives
- Chef's carving knives (I recommend several)
- Kitchen shears
- Paring knife

Nice to Have
- Chopping knife
- Boning knife
- Cleaver
- Serrated bread knife

For the Gourmet-Inclined
- Knife block and knife sharpener

Small Appliances

Essentials
- Food processor
- Blender
- Coffee grinder
- Coffeemaker
- Electric beater
- Microwave oven
- Toaster oven
- Can opener

Nice to Have
- Electric knife (for turkey carving)
- Bread machine
- Espresso maker
- Juicer
- Hand mixer
- Rice cooker/steamer
- Waffle iron
- Slow cooker
- Electric skillet

For the Gourmet-Inclined
- Espresso maker
- Minichopper
- Electric mixer
- Fondue set
- Pressure cooker
- Food mill
- Ice-cream maker
- Pasta machine with ravioli attachments
- Panini machine (for the best-tasting sandwiches on earth)

Baking Accessories

Essentials (they're all nice to have *and* essential!)
- Glass mixing bowls (a set of small, medium, and large)
- Stainless-steel mixing bowls (a set of small, medium, and large)
- Wire whisk
- Measuring cups and measuring spoons
- Insulated cookie sheet
- Flour sifter
- Pastry brushes (small, medium, and large)
- Rolling pin
- Muffin pans, two large and two minis
- Rubber and metal spatulas
- Springform pan
- Round cake pans
- Loaf pan
- Casseroles
- Ovenproof baking dishes

For the Gourmet-Inclined
- Soufflé ramekins
- Bundt pan
- Pizza stone
- Basting brush

Serving Accessories

Essentials
- Wooden salad bowl
- Pasta bowl
- Oval serving platters, two large and two small
- Serving trays (you can never have too many)
- Serving utensils, including serving fork and spoon, and a pasta fork
- Pitcher
- Tongs
- Bread basket
- Coasters (a dozen will do)
- Creamer and sugar
- Butter dish

For the Gourmet-Inclined
- Gravy boat
- Cake plate, with or without lid
- Cake knife

Linens

Essentials
- Dish towels
- Dishcloths
- Pot holders
- Linen napkins (and their stylish cousin, a collection of napkin rings)
- Place mats
- Tablecloths
- Table runners
- Table pad

For the Budget- or Space-Challenged

I haven't always been fortunate enough to live in a spacious Manhattan loft. There have been times in my life when I've been squeezed for room, squeezed for cabinets, squeezed for just about everything (except, of course, style!). I remember living on 54th Street and having a small galley kitchen. Although crammed for space, I still had twelve over for dinner and served a delicious stew or a curry—a one-pot wonder, with a big dose of chic! If you're a recent college graduate, or a couple just starting out in a city where space is hard to come by, here are a few essentials to start you off on an elegant foot.

- Four to six place settings, along with matching silverware
- A microwave oven
- A toaster
- A coffeemaker
- A nonstick 10-inch saucepan
- One or two frying pans, large and small
- A food processor or blender
- A hand or electric beater
- A colander
- A can opener
- Oven mitts
- Chef's carving knives
- Four to six steak knives
- A set of glass and stainless-steel mixing bowls
- A wire whisk
- A measuring cup
- One to two ovenproof baking dishes
- Wine/bottle opener
- Tea kettle
- Garlic press
- Vegetable/potato slicer
- Pepper grinder
- Salad spinner
- Wooden spoons
- Kitchen timer
- Two to three trivets/hot pads
- Cutting board
- Wooden salad bowl
- One to two serving trays
- Serving utensils
- Pitcher
- Four to six place mats
- One to two great-looking tablecloths

Miscellaneous Kitchen Essentials

- Wine/bottle opener
- Tea kettle
- Garlic press
- Vegetable/potato slicer
- Pepper grinder
- Salad spinner
- Scissors and butcher string
- Kitchen timer
- Slotted spoon
- Wooden spoons
- Ladle
- Trivets/hot pads
- Cutting board
- Thermometer
- Citrus reamer/zester
- Salt/pepper mill
- Candles (of different shapes and heights)

Colin's Vinaigrette

- A great salad dressing requires the proper amount of oil in relation to vinegar. I find the ideal ratio to be 4 to 1, or four parts oil to one part vinegar or lemon juice, or whatever you choose to use as your acidic flavor, with a generous amount of salt and pepper. If you want a lighter dressing, use vegetable oil. If you want something with a nutty taste, try hazelnut or walnut oil. And if you want an unsurpassed extra dose of decadence, splurge on some white truffle oil! But change the proportions to ¼ cup truffle oil and ¾ cup vegetable oil to ¼ cup vinegar, since truffle oil is potent!

- For flavoring, add generous pinches of salt and pepper, plus a tablespoon of good-quality Dijon mustard and a finely chopped raw shallot. The options are limitless. If you don't want shallot, and prefer your dressing more pungent and hearty, add a clove of minced garlic instead. If you want a sweeter dressing, sprinkle in a half tablespoon of sugar or honey. For a richer dressing, puree an artichoke heart or add a tablespoon of Stilton cheese; the result is a rich and creamy dressing. No matter what salad greens you're serving, the basic recipe—four parts oil to one part vinegar, salt, pepper, a tablespoon of Dijon mustard, and a well-chopped shallot—always remains the same.

- Every time you reach for my basic vinaigrette, you get a different and delicious variation on the same recipe just by adding a few of the ingredients listed above. Use the basic dressing as a salad dressing, a glaze for baked or barbecued chicken, or a wonderful marinade for shrimp. Drizzle it over grilled seafood, add a zesty touch to winter greens, lentils—your imagination is the limit. Adjust as desired, shake, and you've got four parts delicious to one part fabulous!

The Well-Stocked Refrigerator

If great meals are works of art, then the ingredients inside your refrigerator and the contents of your kitchen cabinets serve as your palette. These are the essentials I recommend everybody keep cold and handy:

- Salad ingredients (a fresh head of lettuce, one or two ripe tomatoes, a bundle of spring onions, chives, parsley, garlic, and shallots) and a squeeze bottle of freshly made salad dressing (see the Colin's Vinaigrette sidebar, previous page).

- Several containers of yogurt (so I can whip up a breakfast smoothie at a moment's notice, or garnish a delicious homemade or store-bought soup with a generous dollop).

- Condiments, including bottled lemon juice; soy or tamari sauce; Tabasco sauce; and assorted chutneys, relishes, jellies, and jams. With a selection of flavors, I can magically doctor whatever meal comes to mind, whether it's takeout or made from scratch. No matter what I'm preparing, I can sweeten it, sour it, salt it, or make it deliciously piquant.

- Fresh fruits, including lemons, limes, and seasonal berries.

- A dozen eggs.

- Milk and butter.

- Two bottles of white wine, a bottle of bubbly, and a selection of beers.

- Bottled water, both flat and sparkling.

- An assortment of cheeses of different textures. A well-rounded selection should include a goat cheese like a chèvre; a creamy cheese, such as Brie or Camembert; a hard cheese like an aged Parmesan or Cheddar; and a pungent cheese, such as a rich blue (Roquefort, Gorgonzola, or Stilton).

"Never wanting to be unprepared, I'm always ready for an impromptu gathering."

Cheese, Please

In France, cheese is typically served before, or sometimes in lieu of, dessert. Across the English Channel, hosts will generally serve it after dessert. Americans most commonly reverse the process by offering cheese as an appetizer during cocktails. It's always fun at a large party to offer a big cheese buffet, including a variety of hard, soft, and creamy cheeses. Always serve cheese at room temperature to ensure the proper consistency and the full flavor. Crusty chunks of baguette, delicious crackers, fava beans, walnuts, honey, and flavored jelly all elegantly complement the flavors of cheeses. If you're serving a tray full of cheese and fruit, I recommend serving a single fruit instead of an assortment because the plate will look cleaner and present more elegantly. My favorites are strawberries, figs, apples, and Champagne grapes.

For an added dose of elegance, serve three or four slices of different cheeses on an individual plate as a separate course after the meal. If you're having a cocktail party, you can tray-pass small plates of cheese to each of your guests along with a few crackers or slices of bread.

The following are among the cheeses I simply can't live without:

Stilton—A beige, flaky, very proper, utterly delicious English blue-veined cheese. Enjoy it with port and thin slices of toasted walnut-raisin bread. It also works nicely as a dessert when served with a slice of warm apple pie.

Saint André—Extremely rich and extremely mild, this luscious triple crème is one of France's most famous and beloved exports.

Taleggio—A very soft cow's milk cheese from Italy's Lombardy region, Taleggio has a rich, piquant flavor that beautifully complements crackers and a crusty baguette.

Pecorino—A wonderfully sharp, salty, robust Italian sheep's milk cheese with a slightly fruity tang and a pale yellow interior. Pecorino is also in huge demand as a grating cheese over pasta.

Chèvre—A soft, chalk-white cheese made from goat's milk that is typically packaged in log shapes, either plain or rolled in ash. It can also be flavored with lemon, paprika, herbs, blue cheese, sometimes even a dusting of semisweet chocolate!

Feta—A classic Greek curd cheese in brine, with a tangy, salty, utterly unmistakable flavor. Its crumble-worthy consistency ranges from very soft to very hard.

Explorateur—A soft, white, decadent, triple crème cheese of unsurpassed delicacy, richness, and flavor. It's worth every single calorie!

Pont l'Évêque—Plump, golden, softly textured and flavorful, it goes wonderfully with full-bodied red wines, cider, or the legendary apple brandy known as Calvados that originates in the same region of France, Normandy.

Tomme de Savoie—Made with skim milk rather than cream, this semi-firm cow's milk cheese with a distinctive gray rind is low in calories and possesses a soft, mild, slightly salty taste.

Manchego—A delectable Spanish sheep's milk cheese that has an intense taste and crumbly texture, making it the perfect accompaniment to a slice of bread, or served in cubes with antipasti.

Cold as Ice: Freezer Fundamentals

The freezer isn't just a place for long-forgotten leftovers. It plays an important role in your entertaining palette. Here are some of the things I keep inside mine:

- Packaged vegetables. Corn, peas, carrots, and fava and lima beans can serve as inspired, last-second additions to stews, pasta, and other dishes.

- Steaks (in various cuts) and chickens. Because I entertain a great deal, I buy my food in bulk. For instance, I probably have twelve organic chickens in my freezer at any given time! Meats and poultry should be wrapped in plastic wrap, then placed in dated freezer bags to guard against freezer burn. They'll taste great for up to three months.

- Soups, stews, and chili. Once in a while I whip up a big pot of homemade soup or a delicious stew, which I then freeze and vacuum-seal in portions custom-ready for two. If I don't have time to make them myself, I stock up on my favorite store-boughts.

- Chicken stock and veal stock. These two bases are the fundamental secrets of the world's most famous chefs and are great for assembling an amazing spur-of-the-moment soup or tasty sauce to go alongside steak, chicken, or lamb. Veal stock works well for rich gravies, especially with some red wine added to the mix. Stocks can be stored in the freezer for up to two months, and will, without a doubt, make your lamb, beef, or pork "gourmet."

- Frozen appetizers. Sausage rolls and samosas can be popped into the oven, or deep-fried, at a moment's notice and served with dipping sauces. If friends drop by unexpectedly, you'll be prepared.

- Chilled vodka or tequila. You never know when there's going to be a great reason to celebrate at a moment's notice, so keep a bottle of vodka or tequila ready and waiting. White wine and champagne can be placed in the freezer one to two hours in advance of your guests' arrival. If they're left too long or forgotten, the cleanup will be messy!

- A selection of frozen yogurt, ice creams, and sorbets.

- Puff pastry. An essential ingredient for quick and easy appetizers.

- Bread and rolls. They last for months and can be quickly toasted or heated in the oven and served hot alongside salads, soups, and your main course.

- Regular and decaffeinated coffee. They'll also last for months in the freezer and you'll never find yourself dragging again.

- Ice! If you don't have an ice maker, I recommend you keep a pound or more in Ziploc bags!

Up, Up, and Away: Cupboard Basics

My kitchen cupboards are ready for anything. You, too, will benefit from stocking up so you'll be ready with a canister of nuts waiting to be toasted for a salad or snack, a package of pasta for a quick fix, the elements of a stew or soup, a package of store-bought meringues for a two-minute dessert, or all of the above. Here's my basic list of necessities:

- Canned tomatoes, tomato sauce, tomato paste, and tomato juice.

- Chicken stock, beef stock, vegetable stock.

- Garbanzo beans.

- Nuts (all varieties, from almonds to unsalted peanuts to macadamias).

- Crackers and Ezekiel bread for snacking, sandwiches, or as an accompaniment to a cheese course or appetizer.

- Pastas (buckwheat and flour) in assorted shapes and sizes.

- Rice: brown, wild, and Arborio.

- Tea, both regular and decaffeinated.

- Flour.

- A selection of peppers, including different-colored pep-percorns. Each has a different flavor.

- A variety of rock salts and sea salts, which are the princi-pal flavoring ingredient most of us use on our foods. Sea salts add extra flavor and texture. A fine salt is saltier to the palate than a coarse salt, and once you've tasted one or two, I promise you'll never go back to the more popular commercial brands.

- A tiered, well-organized shelving system of alphabetized herbs and spices, including oregano, rosemary, thyme, parsley flakes, garlic salt, herbes de Provence (you can find this spice mix at many gourmet stores, if not at your

local supermarket), paprika, coriander, cumin, and cayenne pepper.

- Sugar (granulated, confectioners', and brown, both light and dark).

- Olive oil, extra-virgin olive oil, peanut oil, vegetable oil, walnut oil, truffle oil.

- Balsamic vinegar, red wine vinegar, rice wine vinegar, sherry vinegar.

- Dijon mustard, grain mustard, and spicy English mustard.

The Well-Stocked Cocktail Bar

Finally, no house is complete without these stemware and barware essentials for a spur-of-the-moment cocktail party. I recommend keeping all varieties of the glasses listed below. If you don't have room, collect a smaller number of each, and feel free to mix and match!

- Old-fashioned glasses (12)
- Martini glasses (8)
- Brandy snifters (8)
- Champagne flutes (12)
- White-wine glasses and red-wine glasses or all-purpose wine glasses (16 each)
- Glass pitcher (1)
- Silver ice bucket and ice tongs (1)
- Crystal wine decanters (2)
- Cocktail shaker (1)

white wine
8 oz.

red wine
12.5 oz.

champagne
6 oz.

martini
6 oz.

highball
8–12 oz.

rocks
8 oz.

snifter
17.5 oz.

collins
14 oz.

Liquors and Mixers

- Gin
- Vodka
- Cognac
- Cointreau
- Triple sec
- Champagne
- Red and white wine
- Tequila
- Rum
- A single-malt scotch
- Dry and sweet vermouth
- Bitters
- A selection of traditional cocktail mixers (cranberry juice, ginger ale, 7Up, Coca-Cola, club soda, lime juice, orange juice, tonic water, and some store-bought blends including a great Bloody Mary mix)

"A bottle of bubbly in a silver ice bucket is loaded with chic."

Miscellaneous

- Lemons
- Limes
- Olives
- Sharp knife
- Small cutting board
- Bar towel
- Coasters
- Toothpicks
- Paper and linen cocktail napkins

two

a gracious home: private spaces

A Tranquil Bedroom:
Nightly Rejuvenation

A stylish and well-run home is the sum of more than just the rooms your guests get to wander through. The more intimate areas of your house—the bedroom, the bathroom, and the closet—are just as important as what's seen from the outside.

To be at home, between the sheets, in my own bedroom is one of the most comforting feelings I know. Most people spend nearly one third of their lives in the bedroom, so the space should be as peaceful and luxurious as possible. Your bedroom—and in particular, your bed—is a place for day-dreams, night dreams, and all dreams in between! Bedding today is as exciting as fashion. I happen to like a sleek, tight-looking fitted bed, with crisply ironed pillowcases and sheets. Others may prefer needlepoint pillows and frilly throws. What-ever your taste or preferred style, my one strong recommen-dation: *Never skimp on a mattress and sheets.* They're one of the best investments you'll ever make. You want a mattress that is both supremely comfortable and also provides excel-lent support for aching backs and worn-out muscles. In my bedroom, I have a custom mattress with a Tempur-Pedic pad on top. Next comes the mattress cover and then the über-thread-count sheets, the blanket, and the cover. I also use a contoured Tempur-Pedic pillow. Failing that, you can use a soft down pillow, though with so many people allergic to

goose down, you have to either be discriminating or invest in a pillow made of synthetic down, which won't create dander or mildew.

Until recently, multiple-thread-count sheets were available only at a staggering cost. Now 400- to 800-thread-count bedding can be found at every level of retail from Neiman Marcus to Wal-Mart. Given today's great prices, 400 is the lowest thread count I recommend buying. I also use different sheets at different times of the year. In winter I love sleeping on flannel sheets; in spring or fall, cotton; and in summer there is nothing like lightly starched linen sheets. (The problem with linen is that the sheets are incredibly wrinkled in the morning.)

Your bedroom is a place for sleep and *rejuvenation*. It should reflect your personality in color, mood, fabric, and lighting. Create a look for your bed: sleek, tailored, and hotel-like, filled with comfortable, luxurious pillows. Maybe you like to lay the pillows flat for a modern look, or prop them up for a more traditional feel. Above all, make your bedroom sensuous, inviting, and comfortable.

A Bed for All Seasons

Our bedrooms should be as comfortable as possible, from the dead of winter all the way through the sandy sultriness of summer. The seasons dictate how you should dress the bed and what fabrics to use. Here's a primer:

Summertime

It's hot, sticky, and wonderfully tropical outside, and your bed should look and feel like a light linen suit. Start with the best-quality 100 percent cotton or linen sheets. Layer them with a thin cotton blanket and top that off with a sheet. The result is an inviting hotel-style bed.

Keep a thin wool or cashmere blanket handy for chilly nights or when someone else is controlling the air-conditioning.

If you're a bachelor holding down three jobs, or you're an overworked college student, or you simply decide you don't want to devote the rest of your natural life to ironing, opt for a cotton polyblend that doesn't require any. Make the bed as soon as the sheets come out of the dryer, and they'll look as if you spent hours with iron in hand. Use a fitted bottom sheet and a light cotton comforter.

Spring and Fall

When the snow begins to melt, or the first frost charges the air, bring out a heavier blanket made of wool or a thick-set cotton. If you live in a part of the world where the temperatures fluctuate quite radically during the change of season, place a cashmere fleece or lush flannel blanket at the foot of the bed. You never know when a sudden cold snap will interrupt a sequence of glorious days.

In the Middle of Winter

As with your winter wardrobe, the key to the winter bed is layering. Start with plush flannel sheets and perhaps a soft quilt, and then, of course, comes that comforter, which can be of varying thickness and density of down. I use a heated bed pad—I often sleep with it on—and a soft down comforter. Some people own mattress covers that have different textures on either side—a lightweight cotton surface for the warmer months, and a heavier woolen side for chillier weather. If you own one of these two-faced mattress pads, simply flip the mattress over based on the season at hand.

And if none of the above keep you warm enough, bring out the flannel pajamas and hot chocolate!

Year-Round Comfort

- If you have the time, or you're fortunate enough to have someone preparing and cleaning your bedroom, my number-one choice, from January to December, would be to have ironed sheets on the bed at all times. This isn't as expensive or ultradeluxe a proposition as you might expect. I happen to *adore* fresh sheets, as most everyone does. There is nothing better than the crisp, body-wriggling feel of freshly ironed sheets that have been lightly starched *just so.* A dry cleaner can perform this admittedly tedious task for you, too, or failing that, you can iron them yourself if you have the time and a good book on tape (I find there can be something therapeutic about ironing).

- For a crisp look in no time at all, one good shortcut is to iron just the pillowcases and the top half of the sheet, the portion of the fabric that tucks down at night.

- A second option is to use a decorative bed cover, with a big European pillow stand, and a few decorative pillows and possibly even a neck roll. Pull up the bed cover and you can neatly disguise the unironed sheets! This gives you a bed that is always presentable when the cover and pillows are in place.

- Ideally, you should own two or more sets of everything—sheets, blankets, and pillowcases. While one set is in the wash, the other can be on the bed. To store out-of-season bedding, purchase large, lightweight plastic containers or zipper bags, into which you fold up your winter linens with a sprinkling of cedar chips. They're easy to conceal under a bed or stacked discreetly in a closet.

- Finally, be sure to flip your mattress two to four times a year to keep it looking and feeling as fresh as possible.

"We spend one third of our lives in bed . . . so make it luxurious, comfortable, and über-inviting."

puppy love

Oscar, my adored cocker spaniel, has slept at the foot of my bed his entire life. At this writing, that's nearly nineteen years! To keep the bed clean, I have minicomforters made in the same fabric as the top of my bed cover. If you don't have a bed cover, use a towel, as dogs don't wear lace-up boots, nor do they know how to wipe their feet!

The Well-Dressed Closet

I am always impressed when I shop in stores with clean and orderly shelves where every sweater lines up neatly and all the shirts hang in the same direction. I call this merchandising, and I get so much pleasure out of doing the same thing with my closet. As you take stock of your closet, make sure you have room for everything you need — and a little more. Are you the proud possessor of twenty-five handbags? If so, clear out enough space for thirty! If you're a man with twenty pairs of shoes, leave additional square footage for twenty-five pairs! Measure how many feet you'll need for short-hanging clothes (blouses, shirts, and skirts) and long-hanging clothes (long pants, dresses, and coats). The more orderly and appealing your closet is, the better you'll know at a single glance what your wardrobe options are. Here are a few good tips for organizing your closet:

- Go to any trusted closet manufacturer. The staff can help you determine your specific needs according to what you own, and they will design a custom closet installation that suits you. Home Depot and the Container Store are great options, too.

- Drawer dividers are a necessity. Separate your jewelry, watches, and sunglasses, and especially your underwear. When every one of your closeted possessions has a space, you won't stress or worry about not being able to find your favorite item when you need it!

- Keep a pair of concealed laundry baskets inside your closet — one for dark clothing, the other for light.

- Reserve an area of your closet — a shelf, a drawer, or merely a section of dedicated hanging space — for articles of clothing that aren't dirty but need to be pressed before you can wear them again.

- Install a few pull-out telescoping bars. These allow you to put outfits together effortlessly or even start to pull aside clothing for packing before a trip.

- Consider keeping a locked drawer or safe in your closet for jewels, cash, and passports.

Ruthless Editing: Wear, Love, Give

The golden rule for my closet is this: If I haven't worn a piece of clothing in a year, if I dread the thought of seeing myself in it ever again, if I can't believe I ever bought it in the first place, I give it away to someone who will appreciate it and needs it more than I do.

Right now my wardrobe is smaller than it's ever been. For many years I prided myself on having a vast collection of suits, belts, neckties, and other accessories. Then one day I decided I would pare down my wardrobe to those items that consistently worked for me.

Life is about figuring out where and who you are at any given time, and then continually refining your answers. The decisions you come up with are personal. Figure out what looks magical on you—and what you've outgrown—then rebuild a great wardrobe by judiciously editing the old one. If you buy a new jacket, say good-bye to that old madras one with the sleeves that are just a bit too short. Are six pairs of sneakers cluttering up your closet, when you wear only two? Get rid of the other four.

A ruthless way to edit is to start at one end of your closet and each day move down one piece of clothing, forcing yourself to create an outfit around that piece, and wear it that day. If you don't find anything to go with the top or bottoms you've pulled, consider letting it go. Also, if you wear an article of clothing and don't love it—or just plain feel out of sorts in it—add it to the giveaway pile!

• Find an area in your closet where you can place a tray with a picture frame, a vase of fresh flowers, some fragrant incense, and a small box or bowl for your keys. Failing that, a nearby bureau or table can perform the same decorative function.

Clothing Care: The Basics

• Sort by color and fold clothing properly, from button-down shirts to T-shirts to sweaters. Hang all shirts together by color (from white to black, left to right). When folding T-shirts, use a clipboard as a template so they stack neatly on the shelf.

• Just as Mommie Dearest said, no wire hangers! Recycle them, or return them to the dry cleaner. Invest in cedar, wooden, or plastic hangers. Make sure they match!

• Men's and women's pants should hang either full length or folded, depending on closet space. Skirts and dresses should be hung, colors coordinated, from short to long and from summer to winter or white to black. Jeans can be neatly folded and stacked on a shelf.

• Treat apparel with the same care and respect with which you treat your body. Let your dry cleaner know in advance precisely how to clean and press your clothes. Polish shoes regularly, and repair heels when necessary. Avoid dry-cleaning matching tops and bottoms separately. Dry-cleaning chemicals can alter and distort color, so it's

How to Fold a T-Shirt

Use this method to fold your T-shirts in record time. You will need a large flat surface and, of course, a pile of T-shirts.

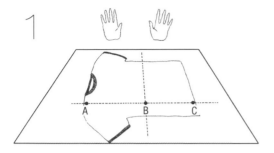

1

Lay the shirt flat and imagine a line running lengthwise down one side of it, and another perpendicular line down the middle. There are three important points on the first line: A, B, and C.

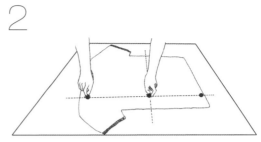

2

Pinch the fabric of the shirt at points A and B, making sure to grab both layers of fabric.

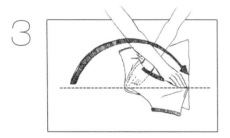

3

Now bring point A to point C, keeping point B stationary. Make sure your arms cross correctly!

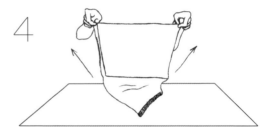

4

Now, with all the layers of fabric of points A and C in one hand, and the fabric of point B in the other, uncross your arms as you lift the shirt off your surface.

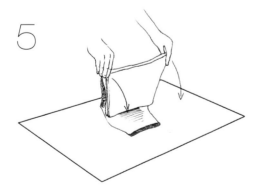

5

Give the shirt a slight shake to straighten it out, then fold the loose side underneath.

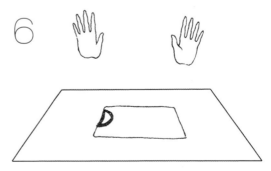

6

Congratulations! The shirt is folded and you're ready for the next one.

best to keep matching pieces cleaned together, even if you're in the habit of only wearing the bottoms!

- Leave your shoes out on a rack and dust regularly. (Keep seasonal shoes in boxes.) Your belts should be hung or rolled neatly in a divided drawer compartment. Neckties can be rolled or hung and assorted by color.

- On top shelves, place storage boxes filled with out-of-season items, such as bathing suits in winter, and gloves, caps, and scarves in summertime. Store anything cashmere in bags with a few cedar balls so the moths don't think they have awakened to an all-you-can-eat buffet!

- Store winter clothes when they are dry. Polish shoes, then wrap in shoe bags before storing. Avoid storing clothing in an area exposed to direct sunlight, because those shirts and blouses closest to the light will fade and have permanent damage. Read the manufacturer's instructions on how to best care for leather bags and purses.

- Like every other room and everything else in life, the closet requires constant maintenance! Spend some time each week keeping it all in place.

In the Closet: Essentials

To walk out the door looking like James Bond or Audrey Hepburn, you need the following closet tools:

- Dedicated drawer for watches and jewelry
- Cubbyholes for purses
- Multiple hooks for necklaces, belts, and hats
- Shoe inserts
- Shoe kit (for a quick shine)
- Shoehorn—a long one with a good handle
- A lint brush
- A clothes brush
- A sewing kit and a box to store all spare buttons
- A travel steamer
- Extra laces
- And, of course, a full-length mirror!

(For more tips on how to create a Swiss-watch–precision closet, see the Home Gallery, pages 116–119.)

Cleanliness Is Divine: The Bathroom

The bathroom is the first room we use in the morning and the last one we use at night, which definitely makes it one of the most important rooms in the house. To me, it's more than just a room with a shower and sink; it's a room where we indulge and refresh ourselves. We can try wonderful spa products and different scents and formulas of scrubs and oils for leisurely baths. We get to shave, arrange our hair, and leave feeling rejuvenated—and looking our very best. Here are a few drab-to-fab bathroom makeovers:

- Soft light is *always* more flattering than harsh, bright white fluorescence. Install a dimmer switch if possible. This way you can control the light level for an efficient morning and the ambience for a romantic night.

- Store your toothbrushes, dental floss, medicines, and other personal items inside the medicine cabinet. Have all bottles, jars, and prescriptions with the labels facing out.

- Use a decanter for mouthwash to add a dash of elegance and get rid of those unappealing plastic bottles!

- Add sexiness by loading up on candles. They create instant atmosphere and invariably soothe your spirit.

- Keep lots of fluffy, high-quality towels on hand. At a minimum, you should have two sets of bath towels, hand towels, washcloths, and face towels. For a casual look, you can roll and place towels in a basket or fold them neatly on a shelf.

- Don't clutter the counter! Accessorize it like a department store's model bathroom. Place a cake of soap on a tray or soap dish or set out a pump dispenser in a shared powder room (it's more convenient and hygienic than a bar of soap). Keep a bottle of hand lotion nearby. A final inspiration: Add something green to your counter (it can be as simple as a vase with a green leaf or a blooming flower).

- A bathroom gets a lot of wear and tear. I'm constantly wiping around the cabinets and sink area, so I keep a cloth towel and some glass cleaner in the cabinet under the sink. (I also like to keep an air freshener within reach, though scented candles and potpourri also get the job done.) Potty 101: As ridiculous as it seems that this isn't just taken for granted, sadly, I have to say the following: As far as the toilet bowl area is concerned, I am addressing the guys here. When men pee, even the most agile sharpshooters can and do miss their marks. My simple suggestion for males everywhere: Be considerate. When you're finished, take a couple of tissues, wipe the edge of the bowl, then flush away the tissue. Whether man or woman, close the toilet seat before leaving the room. I always leave a box of tissues on the toilet cistern. This way they are always on hand for wiping, and they provide great backup if you run out of toilet tissue. Also, make sure there are no stray hairs in the sink!

My Bathroom at 120 Miles an Hour!

There are few more intimate or romantic ways to physically and emotionally reconnect with your partner than a date in the bathroom. I mean it! Spend a night together not out on the town but in the privacy of your own bathroom, relaxing in the tub, pampering yourself and each other.

The sizzling recipe goes as follows: Draw a steaming bath. Using gauze or muslin, make a teabag of eucalyptus and fresh rosemary or any combination of fresh herbs, delicious bath salts, oils, or beads. This turns a soak in the tub into a sensual experience.

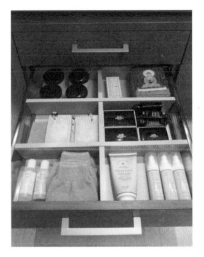

Keep a bottle of bath oil nearby and a bottle of wine or bubbly in an ice bucket within arm's reach.

- Hook up your iPod with tunes to match your mood.

- Finally, it's all about lighting. Dim the lights and let the candles, music, and Champagne take effect while you inhale deeply and relax.

- Afterward, use copious amounts of rich rehydrating body lotion.

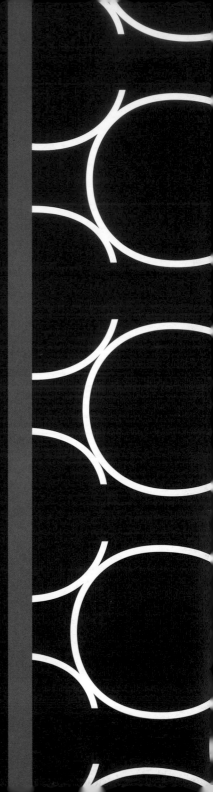

lather, rinse, repeat, renew

However well-placed natural ingredients have their own hard-held charms, a variety of so-called "slick" food, shampoos, creams, and lotions. I concentrate here and therefore on my skin by scrubbing and exfoliating at least three times a week, sometimes more if I've spent a lot of time outside in the sun.

Using body scrub invigorates and replenishes your skin, keeping it looking as youthful as possible. There are some amazing products on the market. But if you're feeling inspired to make your own, here are a few worthy very own homemade recipes.

coffee body scrub

- 2 cups of coarsely ground coffee
- ¼ cup raw sugar or sea salt
- 2 to 3 tablespoons massage oil

Mix all ingredients together. Take a hot shower to moisten your skin and open your pores. Turn off the water and, using wide, circular motions, rub the coffee exfoliant onto your skin with strong, even pressure. Leave it on for fifteen minutes, shower off, pat skin dry, and apply a thin layer of your favorite body lotion.

invigorating almond body glow

For an invigorating rather than relaxing tonic to soft skin, try this traditional Thai recipe.

- 1 cup runny honey
- ½ cup ground almond
- A sprinkling of dried herbs, such as lavender leaf and mint

Shower first, then mix the ingredients together and rub the thick, sticky paste over your body. Take the time to properly exfoliate your skin and make the most of the sweet aroma. (I recommend ten to fifteen minutes). Shower off, pat skin dry, and apply a thin layer of your favorite body lotion.

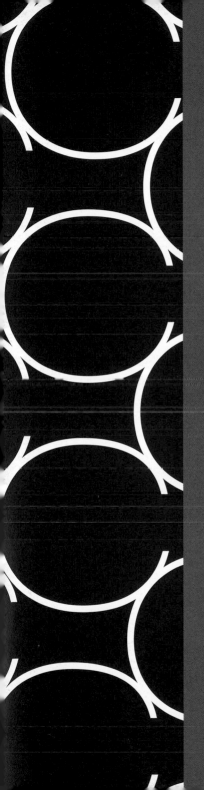

cucumber wrap for sunburn

honey oatmeal facial scrub

"Life is like a bank account.
You can't always take out.
You've also got to put back in."

The Utility Room:
Form Follows Function

Many houses or apartments I've visited have what I like to call a "messy room." These are the functional spaces, basements, attics, out-of-the-way rooms, or even large closets where people store their washing machine and dryer, their cleaning products, their extra house supplies (batteries, paper towels, additional rolls of toilet paper), and maybe even a second refrigerator or freezer to handle the kitchen overflow. A package of sponges sits over here, two boxes of detergent and bleach over there, countless unmatched socks fill a box — in fact, sometimes the amount of chaos in these spaces could rival that of a war zone!

Whether your messy room is a cellar, a side room, or an oversized cabinet, this is how to create one that functions optimally:

- Stay ahead of the mess. Don't let a week's worth of dirty laundry accumulate. Keep the energy moving forward, whether it's the washing machine washing, or the dryer drying. If you do a little bit all the time, you won't end up confronting a mountain of unwashed towels, T-shirts, and pants. Keep dirty clothes inside a container with a well-fitting lid. This allows you to "hide" the mess. But don't ignore the fact that it's there!

- Fold your napkins and towels, underwear, jeans, and T-shirts as soon as the dryer goes off. Take them out of the dryer when they are still warm to the touch. They'll be almost wrinkle-free and will fold more easily — this is a time-saving tip that makes a difference.

- Create a space for everything. Invest in plastic containers, which are available at any department or container store and can be neatly stacked and arranged by contents and category. I compartmentalize everything. This way I don't waste time searching for a pair of double-A batteries or a few extra hangers. I also make sure my containers are clearly marked, with their labels facing out. Use a label maker for consistency. Place the following in labeled containers:

the gift closet or cupboard: instant grace — a must-have today

Whenever I'm going over to someone's home or apartment for the evening, I like to bring along a gift. It might be some chic presentation of incense, a wrapped bottle of interesting wine, a compilation of music, or something special I've picked up from one of my trips abroad.

They are all prewrapped, and thanks to small, removable labels, I know what's inside each box. I have a couple of plastic containers that are gift related; they hold paper, tape, ribbons, and gift cards. This way I can get out the door, gift in hand, at a moment's notice.

- Sponges
- Shoe-cleaning supplies
- Shoelaces and accessories
- Batteries (all sizes)
- Sewing kit and supplies
- Silver cleaners
- Laundry soaps, fabric softeners, bleaches
- Extra shampoo, conditioners, and body soaps
- Extra toothbrushes, toothpaste, and dental floss
- Coupons
- Candles and lighters
- Whatever else you have multiples of

- If the garage or basement serves as your storage area, paint everything a neutral color. Line the back wall with a shelving system for storage.

"With self-diagnosed ADD, I thrive on order around me. Everything should have a place."

- If the utility room doubles as a storage area for linens, use a matching shelving system for sheets, blankets, towels, and hand towels. Your linens will look very appealing when arranged like this.

- In my linen storage area, I break down the bedding supplies further. My summer sheets go together in one container, my winter sheets in another. I keep mothballs in one drawer, cedar wood chips in another, and ready-to-sprinkle naphthalene pellets in a third.

- Edit by asking yourself if you will ever *really* wear that old sweater again, or use that Nintendo set. If not, pass it on (see page 78 for some suggestions on how to sell or donate things you no longer use). Instead of storing it, get rid of it.

Suggestion: I recommend Shaklee's green cleaning products for many home uses. The company is owned by my friend Roger Barnett. I've recently replaced all my cleaning products with Shaklee's, which allow us to live in a healthier environment, protect and clean our homes efficiently, and, most important, have the lowest possible impact on the planet.

colin cowie chic

SOS! Always Be Prepared:
Emergency Essentials

Having lived through California's Northridge earthquake, as well as September 11 in New York, not to mention countless power outages here and abroad, I know it's essential to be well prepared. Here's a list of necessities that will help shepherd you through most emergencies:

- Keep cash at your disposal in small denominations. In the event of a national disaster or quarantine, most banks will close—and that includes ATMs. The same applies in the event of a power outage. In such an environment, money will revert to its most primitive form, as the basis of the official and universal system of bartering.

- Keep in storage several gallons of water as well as a good-sized supply of canned food (tuna fish, peanut butter, chicken stock, canned tomatoes, and so forth) and protein bars. If there's a national or regional quarantine, you should have enough food and water to get you through five days. And don't forget your pet's needs! (Remember what happened to the Hurricane Katrina victims in 2005.)

- Keep close by a working first-aid kit, a battery-operated transistor radio (in case the electrical power goes out), and a flashlight, as well as an extra set or two of batteries.

- If possible, keep an extra set of your medication around, particularly if you're someone with a chronic condition like diabetes.

- If you live in Southern California or another earthquake zone, store in the back of your car a backpack containing these same items, plus an anorak and some running or walking shoes. You could be miles away from home when a disaster strikes.

- Finally, with friends and family make a concrete and prearranged plan or communications system that you can call upon in case of emergency. After 9/11, several of my friends got together, and we exchanged telephone numbers and decided that if something like that ever happened again, we would meet at a specific, agreed-upon location—in this case, a friend's apartment close to the 59th Street (or Queensboro) Bridge, in case we had to evacuate Manhattan. Make sure you spell out your plan in as detailed a way as possible; then keep everybody in the loop.

Oscar and Me: A Love Story

Nineteen years ago my sister Janet, visiting from South Africa, arrived carrying the most adorable cocker spaniel puppy in her arms. I fell in love, and in my modest and completely unbiased opinion, Oscar can do absolutely no wrong. I do believe in life after death, and hope in my next life to come back as Oscar! I've done everything within my power to make him human and instill in him what I call "petiquette"!

- I never bring Oscar with me to friends' homes unless it's cleared beforehand. This includes casual drop-by visits and (most emphatically) overnight stays.

- Schedule your dog to be washed once every few weeks, the same for a cutting. Don't forget to brush his teeth on a regular basis. A clean, well-groomed dog is a happy dog.

- Train your pet not to jump on people or put his or her wet face and nose on a guest's lap.

- No begging, ever! There are few things worse than a begging dog, especially at the dinner table.

- Use a lint remover or double-sided tape daily to remove dog and cat hair from furniture and clothing.

- Wash your pet's bowls daily—you don't eat off dirty dishes; why should your dog or cat?

- Reward good behavior with a treat, and acknowledge bad behavior firmly the moment it happens. Don't blame the dog for making an accident in the hallway if you've forgotten to walk him in four hours!

- Crate training is a great idea, but it shouldn't be abused. Don't keep your dog in a cage for long hours.

- Animals are an enormous responsibility, and there is nothing worse than cruelty to them. If you witness cruelty, immediately call the ASPCA or your local animal welfare office.

- Never let children torment your pets. A dog who snaps can't really be blamed if someone has been yanking his tail for the past half hour.

- Never give someone a pet as a present unless you've cleared it beforehand!

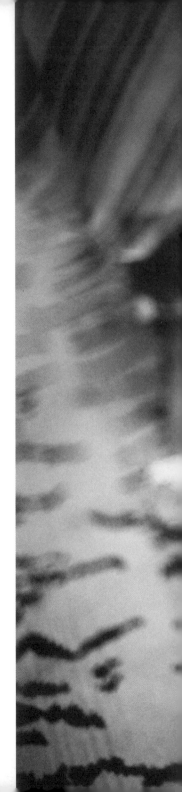

good-bye, old pal: putting a pet down

It can be one of the most traumatic experiences on earth. If you're faced with this difficult decision, here are a few things to keep in mind:

- Make your pet's final hours anxiety-free. It's better to have a doctor come to your house than put your animal through the stress of driving to the vet's office. Find out if your local veterinarian is willing to make house calls.

- For the last meal, spoil your pet with a wonderful, juicy, rare filet mignon or other favorite treat, and whatever delicious finger foods you know will be enjoyed.

- When it's time for the vet to give your pet the shot, take your dog or cat in your arms, look straight into those eyes, and talk in a gentle, loving voice. This is the last time you'll see each other, so make your words count. This will bring enormous comfort and closure to both you and your pet.

The Staff of Life: Household Employees

It's a luxury to have domestic help, and I'm one of the lucky ones. My housekeeper Gertrude has been with me for more years than both of us care to remember; I respect her enormously and treat her with the same courtesy I would expect if I were working for her. In general, it's been a tremendous source of pride to me that I have *never* had a problem with my domestic help, be it Gertrude or any of the people who worked with me before her. In fact, I must be doing something right, because from all appearances, my staff can't seem to do enough for me and are always only too happy to go the extra mile to make sure I'm happy with their work (which makes them proud, too).

I can think of five good reasons why:

1. I make my needs, desires, and expectations crystal clear.

2. Most people have the right hardware . . . and it's up to the employer to install the correct software.

3. I use incentives to motivate my staff.

4. The people in my employ don't work *for* me; they work *with* me.

5. I maintain proper boundaries at all times.

Let me elaborate:

- First, I always want to make certain that I'm hiring legal workers. Aside from the legal and liability issues, illegal aliens are exactly that—illegal—and hiring them is illegal, too. I make sure I have copies of all my household employees' Social Security numbers, driver's licenses, and passports. In the worst-case scenario, if something goes terribly wrong, I know where to start looking. (A note about illegal workers: If you meet someone you'd like to hire to work for you, but his or her documentation isn't in order, consider sponsoring that person to help them get the proper papers. It's a lengthy process, but worth the investment in helping someone who is seriously devoted to bettering his or her life.)

- When I hire a household employee, I'm hiring that person in a professional capacity. Therefore, I spell out in writing precisely what I expect: the working hours; the salary; days off; morning, afternoon, and evening duties; and weekly and monthly responsibilities.

- If your employee doesn't have a good command of English, take digital photographs and place them in a book. Show your employee how a beautifully made bed should look and what foods and beverages you always want to see inside your refrigerator. Rarely do I come across people who aren't eager to do an excellent, responsible job — but one cannot expect staff members to be mind-readers or psychics.

- Motivate your employees. Here's one fail-safe means of motivation that I have discovered over the years and that works like a charm (though I admit it can be out of reach for people who don't travel for work as much as I). As a person who flies around the world a great deal, I earn a tremendous amount of free airline mileage per year. Consequently, I'm in the fortunate position to tell my employees the following: "If at the end of the year I'm happy with your work, you and a companion can fly anyplace in the world — my treat." Can you imagine what an extraordinary incentive and inducement this is? If this is beyond your means, consider more modest variations: a dinner for two at the restaurant of the employee's choice in the town or city where you live, or two tickets to a concert by that person's favorite band.

- With hard work comes gratitude, respect, and rewards. My trusted housekeeper Gertrude works unbelievably hard for me, and I am fair and generous in return. If she works late, I always send her home in a car service. Every year, I give her two weeks off, and some of my airplane miles, so she can take a vacation. After thirteen years, she is a family member and takes care of my home and my possessions as if they were her own. I have tremendous respect for this woman.

Hiring Household Staff

Interviewing and References

Never hire someone solely on the basis of an interview. Call for references. If the person you're interviewing is going to be taking care of your children, then get multiple references. You might also want to hire a private investigator to run a background check to uncover any criminal convictions or drug or credit problems. After all, you're giving this individual full, unconditional access to your home, family, and possessions, so do your homework in advance. If potential employees tell you they know how to cook, ask them to fry an egg, prepare a salad, or grill a steak. If their job responsibilities include making your bed, have them showcase their talents!

What to Expect: Make It Clear

When you hire a housekeeper, spell out clearly what you want (and don't want) in addition to the hours, compensation, and benefits. I recommend a two-week paid trial period, after which the two of you can mutually decide if you want your professional relationship to continue.

In addition to ordinary everyday duties, include side issues such as lateness: "If you're running late because you missed the bus, or your babysitter hasn't arrived, please call." Give out your cell phone, office, and private phone numbers. If you have to leave and need something done, leave clearly written instructions.

Give your employee those responsibilities that will free you up to be more productive in your own life—picking up and dropping off dry cleaning, grocery shopping for staples, walking the dog—then clearly state all these duties and responsibilities when you are interviewing someone. For good measure, outline them in a written schedule.

Creating a Contract

Put everything in writing. Include your employee's telephone number and home address, Social Security number, driver's license number, and a copy of their passport.

Suggestion: If your housekeeper or nanny will be driving your children or running errands on your behalf, make sure he or she has the proper license and necessary insurance. Check your employee's driving record with his or her current insurance company, or if you're planning to take care of the insurance, your company will do it for you when they give you a quote.

If It Doesn't Work Out

If the trial period went poorly, or if there's any reason to distrust the employee, or damages have occurred, document the situation (take photographs, for example) and give your employee one or two warnings before, if necessary, dismissing them. State in writing the reasons for the dismissal and have the employee sign it, should you ever be taken to court for wrongful dismissal, which is commonplace. Some states are "at-will" employment states, which means hiring and firing can be done without cause; others aren't and require compliance with state laws. Know which laws apply to you!

Once a household employee is dismissed, he or she should leave as soon as possible, if not immediately. Pay out two weeks' severance salary, or whatever is fair given the situation. Whether a household employee is leaving under pleasant or unpleasant circumstances, if they've had access to your charge accounts at the liquor store, grocery store, pharmacy, or hardware store, make sure you fax or e-mail each store a letter informing them that you have rescinded that individual's access. Call to verify the managers' receipt of the fax. Have a locksmith change all the locks. Alter any passwords or PINs your former employee may have known about or memorized. Always inform your security company or building personnel about any changes in household staff.

Eco-Conscious Living:
Green Is Clean

With unseasonably warm winters and a spate of stories about how our actions are changing the environment, it's time to think about what we can do to stop global warming. Here are some strategies to give this planet a fighting chance!

1. Consider going green. Cleaning supplies, paper products, and other household essentials that are environmentally friendly, or "green," are available at most major markets and department stores. Usually, they're clearly labeled, but if in doubt, stop by your nearest Whole Foods store. From organic cottons to dishwashing liquids, a little detective work is all it takes! And whenever possible, buy in bulk. This isn't merely convenient and time-saving; it also saves on packaging that you'll eventually throw away.

2. Limit or even eliminate your use of plastic bags. They are generally not biodegradable and do not decompose thoroughly. If your purchase is small, either skip the bag, or do as many Europeans do and bring along your own canvas sack. Most stores sell bags like these today or give them away with their brands plastered all over them.

3. Recycle all your paper, glass, and plastic products. If there is no recycling program in your building or neighborhood, use the Internet to find the recycling center nearest you.

4. Fix leaky faucets, which can waste up to twenty gallons of water a day, and running toilets, which can waste up to a hundred gallons a day. Turning the faucet off while you brush your teeth can save gallons of water per minute!

5. Buy a low-flow showerhead for your bathroom. This will cut your water consumption by almost 50 percent! Soaping down in the shower? Turn off the water until you're ready to rinse.

"I think being conscious of the environment should be our #1 priority. I do whatever I can in my home and office and inspire my staff and friends to do their best in their homes and offices."

Sell It, Donate It, Swap It

There's no need to throw away things or waste something that could benefit others. Here are some great ways to sell an item, give it away, or exchange it:

- To sell an object, consider running a classified ad in your local newspaper, or go to http://www.craigslist.com to publicize items that you no longer have any use for.

- Don't forget eBay. If you choose to sell an object by yourself on eBay, be aware that the company's pricing structure is typically 5.25 percent (details can be found at http://pages.ebay.com/help/sell/fees.html). If you haven't the time or the inclination to conduct your own eBay auction, go to http://www.i-sold-it.com, a national outlet that does all the work for you, including photographing, listing, selling, packing, and shipping your unused merchandise to the winning eBay buyer. Their take is typically one third of the winning bid for the first five hundred dollars, and one fifth of the remaining amount.

- To exchange or donate merchandise, go to http://www.freecycle.org, a wonderful nationwide volunteer site that offers local community online bulletin boards. You can list merchandise you would like to get rid of, and you can check out various items you might need. Best of all, the person who wants the item is responsible for pickup!

- National and local charities are also great places to give away your unwanted stuff. Call a favorite charity to find out how to make a donation.

"I believe in absolute generosity 100 percent of the time, and would rather die with less, knowing that I've shared with everyone along the way."

6. Turn your thermostat down one degree, and your heating costs will immediately decrease. And, of course, lower your thermostat if you're going away for the weekend. Keep your air conditioner at a respectable temperature. There's no reason to suffer, but there's no reason to be wasteful, either (no one needs to sleep in a meat locker!).

7. Almost two hundred thousand tons of batteries end up in the garbage every year. The metals inside them can seep into the earth, threatening our water supplies. Reduce your use of batteries by using electric sources whenever possible—or by investing in rechargeable batteries.

8. Put an end to the mountains of junk mail you receive every day by logging on to http://www.dmaconsumers.org/consumerassistance.html. The DMA is a trade organization for marketing companies that send out catalogs and mailings. You can request to be taken off mailing lists, and the DMA's members must adhere to the organization's standards (and consumers' wishes) in order to maintain their membership.

9. Avoid aerosol sprays. You can't recycle their cans, which means that they're destined for a landfill near you, and many of their ingredients contribute to air pollution, too. Shop instead for dispenser bottles, liquids, powders, and roll-ons.

10. Unplug! Appliances such as cell phone rechargers, TVs, and VCRs still draw energy—and cost Americans up to a billion dollars a year in electricity!

three

inviting guests into your home: stay for a while

How to Be a Great Host

Inviting guests into your home is all about making them feel welcome and well cared for. I love having company and sharing with them the pleasures of delicious food, a pitcher of martinis, a beautiful table, a great new CD I've just discovered —or all of the above.

Some people host overnight visitors on a futon in the living room, or on a blow-up mattress, or on a rollaway in the den. Others are fortunate enough to have an elaborate guest suite with all the trimmings. It hardly matters, as long as you make your guests comfortable. In my Miami apartment, for example, I use a sofa bed in the den for out-of-town guests. In my New York apartment, I have a separate guest bedroom. But in both locations I take enormous pleasure in making up the bed with my ironed and lightly starched sheets, setting up the bedside table with a carafe of ice water and a glass, lighting a candle, and at night, turning down the sheets. I enjoy staying up late at night talking with good friends, or conducting a conversation with my guest as we're both walking my dog. But regardless of what kind of guest room you have, the most important elements by far are comfort and a sense of genuine welcome.

Preparing a Welcoming Guest Room

When you enter my guest bedroom, you can't help but want to stay awhile, or move in permanently! I only invite close friends and family to stay in my house, and I go all out to make my guests' visit as relaxing as possible. I like to think of myself as running a little hotel or inn. As my late father once explained, "Colin, you don't have people stay in your house unless you treat them like a king or a queen." Like father, like son, I will *always* go that extra mile. I place myself in my guest's shoes. On one or two occasions I've gone over to people's houses or apartments, and they were still getting ready for my arrival, which always makes me feel slightly awkward in an oh-no-you-shouldn't-bother way. Ideally, if I were staying the night at a close friend's house, I'd want to feel welcomed, appreciated, and thoroughly prepared for. I want to be waiting for my houseguests so that when they arrive, they feel right at home—and not as though they are a burden or an imposition.

A few touches you might follow when rolling out the red carpet for houseguests:

- All the comforts my guests could want await them in the guest bedroom, including a dimmer switch for the lights, a TV, a DVD player, some interesting reading material (my favorite books, a couple of current magazines), and a bowl of delicious dates, candy, or fresh fruit. You could place a chocolate on the pillow, but every hotel has done that already!

- If you're having your guests take over a room that's usually occupied, or if they're sleeping in a den, make space for them and clean up the area around the bed, particularly the bedside table. Empty out one or two drawers, and supply extra wooden hangers for the closet.

- Whatever kind of bed you have, whether it's a single, double, king, queen, pull-out couch, or a futon, it should look and feel as inviting and as luscious as possible. If it's a bed, provide at least the same quality mattress in your guest room as you use in your own bedroom.

Sample Welcome Notes

I use this note to welcome my guests.

Dear Donna and Tom,
Welcome to New York! I'm really looking forward to spending some time together. In order to make your stay as comfortable as possible, I've included a list of a few of my favorite restaurants [with the addresses and telephone numbers of each provided], the name of a florist, a car service, a liquor store (it delivers!), a password should you need to log on to the wireless system, the house phone and fax numbers and my contact numbers. Let's make this one to remember! Love, Colin

Sometimes I will handwrite a personal note that reads simply:

Welcome to my house. I'm looking forward to our next couple of days and happy that you and I get to reconnect. Love, Colin

You might also take this opportunity to give your guests a rundown of your upcoming week, including your work schedule, so they can plan their lives accordingly.

I've made arrangements for us to be together for dinner at a fun new restaurant on Wednesday at 8:30 P.M. I will be cooking on Friday night and have invited a few other friends I know you'll love meeting. Other than that, you're on your own! Here are some of my favorite restaurants in the area, and the best place to find good-quality food after midnight if the mood strikes. Make yourself at home, and try me on my cell phone when you get settled. Love, Colin

Naturally, if the houseguest is your mother or your closest friend on earth, there's no need to write a letter. But you should still communicate the social schedule, and let your guests know they can take it easy.

"There's coffee in the kitchen, fruit in the refrigerator, and please help yourself to whatever snacks you might find in the pantry. In short, make yourself at home!"

- Make the bed up with crisp, clean, and color-coordinated linens. If your guest is arriving in the winter, tuck an extra blanket or comforter in the closet and let him or her know it's there, or leave it folded at the foot of the bed.

- Provide a luggage rack, a bench, or a large bathroom towel where guests can set down their suitcases. I do whatever I can to make sure the luggage never directly touches the clean blanket or linens on the bed. This is the same suitcase or duffel that has just been removed from the hold of an airplane, hurled onto a luggage carousel, dragged through the airport on a cart, and manhandled into the trunk of a taxi cab or limousine. By the time it gets to the bedroom it's pretty filthy!

"I love having guests. It lets me play house. I'm ready 24/7 (check-in is at three!)."

- The bedside table should have all necessities within reach. If there's a telephone on the bedside, turn the ringer to the off position so that if a call comes in early in the morning, it won't disturb your sleeping guests. Keep a notepad and pen beside the telephone—for guests to jot down a name or a number—as well as a working alarm clock, a water carafe and glass on a tray, with a fragrant candle burning when they arrive.

- A well-informed guest is a happy guest. For a very special touch, if you have the time, place on the bed or on the bedside table a welcome letter/folio along with information regarding their visit, attractions of interest in the neighborhood, important phone numbers, and a map.

- Make an extra set of house keys for your guests so they can come and go as they please. Make sure they know the security procedures for your house.

- Another intimate touch: I will find a photograph of my guest and me, preferably one taken during our last visit together. I will place the photo in a frame and leave it next to the bed or on the sideboard, or often I'll gift wrap it as a welcome present for him or her.

- Few things appeal to guests more than a generous-sized closet, with loads of hanging space. If you can't fully empty out the closet of personal belongings, then make it a point to move all your possessions over to one side. By doing this, you let your guest know that they are not an imposition and that you want them to be as comfortable as you can possibly make them. This has nothing to do with the square footage you give them. It is all about making them feel relaxed and welcome.

- For added comfort, provide a comfortable chair in their room or the area where they'll be staying.

- A really chic touch my houseguests always appreciate: Just after dessert, while they are enjoying the last of the wine, I excuse myself while everyone is still chatting and head out to the guest room to fold down the bed cover. I fill the carafe with chilled water, light a candle, and leave a bowl of fresh tangerines or dates by the bed. It takes literally a few minutes of my time, but the results make them feel like a rock star and my guest room five-star!

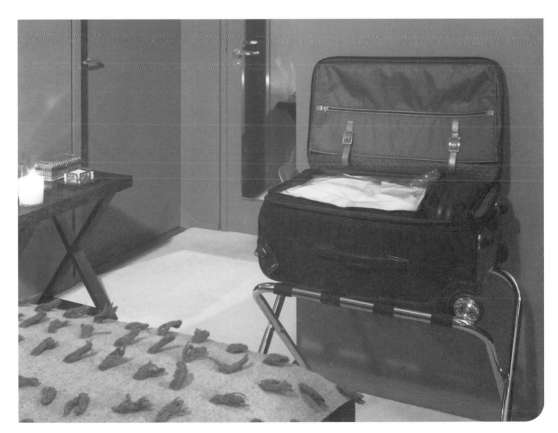

The Guest Bathroom: Basic Requirements

When it comes to the guest bathroom, provide guests with all the practical and luxurious items they may have forgotten to pack, as well as a few extra surprises. Here's a quick checklist that will turn your guest bathroom into a heaven away from home!

- ❏ Toothpaste
- ❏ New toothbrushes in their unopened plastic packaging
- ❏ Dental floss
- ❏ Shaving cream
- ❏ Razors
- ❏ New lip balm
- ❏ Sanitary pads/tampons
- ❏ Cologne and perfume
- ❏ Cake of fresh soap and a jar of exfoliating scrub
- ❏ Shampoo
- ❏ Body lotion
- ❏ One or two sticks of fragrant incense

Other special touches to consider:

- Whenever I travel, I find wonderful amenities in hotel rooms all over the world, which I bring home for use in my guest bathroom. Failing that, a little shopping always yields a harvest of indulgent bath products. My neighborhood grocery and beauty-supply stores also offer great travel-sized necessities. I stock the shower and bath with body wash and scrubs, hair shampoo and conditioner, face cleanser, and a fresh loofah sponge. The point is to always supply your guests with something that hasn't been opened or used. It looks that much more inviting.

- Leave a clean glass and a decanter with mouthwash plus two hand towels and a face towel at the sink. I place the bath towel on the counter or hang it on the towel rack as well. If there's no room, you can place it neatly in the bedroom at the foot of the bed along with another hand towel. A flower on top or a fresh (or even dried) sprig of rosemary will earn you major points! But plush, luxurious quality towels are a must. A good towel has long dense loops and will last several years. If you're sharing a bathroom, let your guests know which towels are yours and which are theirs.

- All year round, my guests will always find a warm, washable floor mat in front of the toilet, and a second mat outside the shower area.

- Another necessity is a full-length mirror. Everyone appreciates a head-to-toe view! Short of space? Place it on the back of the door.

- Your guest bathroom should have a scale. Now that we've gotten a head-to-toe look at ourselves, we need one to make sure our eyes aren't lying.

- If guests are coming in that evening, I'll place a lit fresh candle in the bathroom a half hour before their arrival. Or I'll begin burning a stick of incense so the bathroom smells delicious and inviting when they arrive. Fold the toilet paper into a neat *V* to really make your visitors feel welcome.

- Place a fresh flower (or flowers) in the room. I love the idea of something alive in a room, whether it's a blooming orchid plant, a box of wheatgrass in the spring, a beautiful assortment of freshly cut wildflowers, or a simple tropical leaf.

(For more on how to create a heavenly guest bedroom and bathroom, check out the Home Gallery, pages 123 to 125.)

"How we live in our homes and treat ourselves extends to how we welcome and treat others—and is the essence of true style."

Be a Good Houseguest

It could be as short as an overnight stay . . . or as long as family members paying a visit for the holidays, but the bottom line of mindfulness, courtesy, consideration, and pure passion that defines a great host also applies to a great houseguest! The most important thing to remember is to remain open and communicate with your hosts about your expectations and theirs. Respect their home as much — and even more so — than you do your own. Put yourself in their place! Imagine how gratified you'd feel as a host if a weekend houseguest offered to help out in the kitchen, surprised you with an überglorious bottle of Champagne or an armful of gourmet groceries, and treated every room in your house, and every person in your life, with the utmost respect and gratitude. Being invited to stay in someone's house is a lot more than a convenience. It's an honor and a privilege. Treat it that way, and I guarantee you'll be invited back again and again!

Paving the Way

You score big points when you send a house present ahead of your arrival — flowers, chocolates, or wine, for example — along with a note: "Thank you so much for the invitation to visit. I look forward to spending quality time with you." In second place, arrive with a thoughtful gift such as a compilation CD, a rare bottle of Champagne, a huge bouquet of flowers, or any of the gift ideas above along with a personal note expressing how much you are looking forward to the visit.

Please Come Again!

As the guest, treat your host's home with the utmost respect. You might put your bare feet on the furniture in your own house, but remember, you're not there now! Don't place change or keys on your bedside table, because they may scratch the lacquer or wood finish. If you take a bottle of wine from the refrigerator, buy one or two bottles the following day to replace it. If your stay is an "extended" visit,

will you still be here
at christmas?

Guests turn into a burden only if they're given the opportunity to do so. Both host and guests should be straightforward about the length of the guests' stay *before* they arrive.

then stop by the grocery store and pick up some essentials. (A host shouldn't expect his houseguests to shop for groceries, but if they do it without your knowledge, accept the groceries graciously.) Help clear the table and clean up after dinner. Guests shouldn't expect to be waited on; they should pitch in and help (or at least offer to) whenever possible.

Houseguest Rules

Is Call Forwarding Too Forward?

Yes! It's an imposition on your host to have business or social calls forwarded to his telephone line. Use your cellular phone instead!

In the Bedroom

If your hosts are fortunate enough to have household help, there's no need to make your bed. However, you might want to pull the blankets up over the sheets so that the overall effect is tidy. If there isn't any help, you should make the bed properly in the morning, and leave the bedroom as clean as you found it.

In the Bathroom

Sharing a bathroom? Keep your toiletries in a separate kit and take them in and out of the bathroom as needed. Make sure you leave the bathroom spotless for the next person.

Custody of the Computer

If you haven't brought along your own laptop, ask permission before logging on to your host's computer. Make sure you're not inconveniencing anyone, and try not to spend all day at someone else's desk, Googling your family tree. If you need to print something out, make sure you replace the paper, particularly if you're drafting a sequel to *War and Peace.*

The Great Host . . . and the Guest Who Wants to Be Invited Back

Great hosts . . . make their guests feel welcome and comfortable *always*! They keep all crises at bay. No one wants to walk into a home that's laden with stress.

Guests who want to be invited back . . . let you know in advance when they're arriving and provide you with their various contact numbers. If there are any changes to their schedule, they'll let their hosts know at once.

Great hosts . . . pull out the passion percentage: that extra 20 percent of effort and love. For friends, one should always go that extra mile.

Guests who want to be invited back . . . arrive self-sufficient, so they're as little an imposition as possible. For hygiene's sake, they take off their shoes at the door (or at least offer), and place their toiletries on a hand towel in the bathroom, either on the counter or in a drawer, and not directly on the sink. If the host has emptied out a drawer or cabinet, guests should place their toiletries inside.

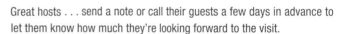

Great hosts . . . may lead staggeringly busy lives, but they take time for great friends, knowing that they're the most valuable assets in life.

Guests who want to be invited back . . . arrange to take their hosts out to dinner one evening—and offer a sincere thank-you toast.

Great hosts . . . send a note or call their guests a few days in advance to let them know how much they're looking forward to the visit.

Guests who want to be invited back . . . send their host a note after their stay. I like to arrange for flowers to be delivered to the host following my departure. If the plane leaves at two in the afternoon, arrange for a floral delivery between three and five, along with a handwritten note addressing the visit, for example, "I'll never drink tequila again without you! This weekend with you was a tonic for my soul." When guests reach their destination, they might e-mail their hosts, telling them they arrived safely.

Checking Your E-Mail

If you need a phone line to send and receive e-mails, whether from a laptop or from your host's desktop computer, clear it with your host before plugging in. Check to see if a dedicated line is available before unplugging any phones from the jack.

Thanks for the (Household) Help

Treat them politely, with respect—and you shouldn't expect them to do more than make your bed and clean your bathroom. However, if the household help has done your laundry, or attended to your dry cleaning, or helped make your meals memorable, put some money in an envelope at the end of your stay along with a thank-you note. Include a small amount of cash for a short stay and more for a longer visit. It all depends on your income—but always err on the side of generosity! Strip your own bed before you leave, folding the linens and used towels and leaving them in a neat pile at the foot of the bed.

Keep It Short and Sweet

If you've arrived with all good intentions, but find that the household energy is suffering due to tension between your hosts, or you simply don't feel welcome, have the wisdom to cut your visit short before you endanger your friendship. Be gracious, and put aside any discussion of the tension you're picking up for another time. "We've been having a wonderful visit with you, but we find ourselves yearning for a bit of private time together. We're hoping you won't mind if we spend the last couple of days of our trip at the hotel down the road. We've loved our stay, but we really need a few days on our own before going home."

If you're a solo guest, there's nothing wrong with some variation of "I find myself yearning for some time alone." It's all in the delivery!

1 A spare, clutter-free entryway sets the right tone for the party that's just around the corner!

2 A mercury-glass installation of pillar candles, reflecting balls, and bowls filled with limes and grapes looks inviting on the dining room table. Fresh fruit provides color inexpensively and lasts a lot longer than fresh-cut flowers.

3 A well-curated collection of flea-market finds makes for an extremely elegant first impression. Fragrant candles add an inviting touch.

1 The entrance to my home is glamorous and überinviting, with warm, soothing lighting, a circular gray mat so guests can wipe their feet, and a curtain of chain-link beads illuminated with colored lights adding a seductive touch (you can't help but reach out and thrum them with your fingers!). Often, I'll scatter a couple of votives in my entrance to make my guests feel even more welcome.

2 I have two separate seating arrangements in my living room, joined by amoeba-shaped ottomans. This works particularly well for smaller gatherings, as well as for twenty or more.

3 When creating seating arrangements in your home, make them as intimate as possible, which paves the way for easy conversation.

3

1 The living room in my previous Upper East Side apartment was decorated in the style of the 1940s. My modus operandi when decorating is to pick one color scheme and use it as a thread of style through everything. A bottle of Champagne and some delicious jumbo shrimp hanging over the edge of a gorgeous 1940s bowl make everybody feel welcome.

2 Browsing in an art store once, I found this incredible copper-foil paint in a two-ounce jar, and I told the owner I needed twelve gallons! By changing the direction of the paintbrush, I created these intricate wall patterns. Best of all, copper-foil paint bathes everyone in the most flattering light, as if they've just come back from someplace fabulous.

3 A very beautiful 1950 starburst pendant light fixture adds sparkle and luster to my table. The draperies are stitched together to match the coloration in the carpet (and don't forget the warm luxuriance of that copper-foil light).

4 This armchair came off the S.S. *Normandy*. I reupholstered the chair in red silk velvet and covered over a window that never provided much light in the first place. Even though the space is very rich and warm, it still has a very modern feeling about it. Once again, focusing on one color makes for a very powerful impression.

5 All I do is switch on the lights . . . and the room becomes glamorously alive. There's nothing quite like the hearth of a fireplace to make you feel at home. Also notice the profusion of the color persimmon. Not bad for a simple boy from Africa!

1 Everyday dining never has to be drab. I always keep it fab with a couple of placemats, some plates I found in Manhattan's Chinatown, some inexpensive reactive-glaze china plates, some regal glass tumblers (they wash well and quickly in the dishwasher), and the centerpiece, which is made of moss balls and candles placed in a tray (tray chic!).

2 As you can see, I've taken the napkin and rolled it in mother-of-pearl, which I found in an inexpensive jewelry mart and used to create a dozen napkin rings. And of course there's no such thing as a dinner gathering without votive candles. Note that I'm using my sterling silver every day, because it belongs in the dishwasher, not in the safe under lock and key!

3 Playing on my African roots, I've used an organic placemat trimmed with seashells. The dishes are inexpensive Columbian pottery, and the pair of tumblers can go straight into the dishwasher.

4 I enjoy dining in the kitchen, and I inject my everyday china and glasses with a shot of glamour, like this snowy white runner and a pair of chunky votive candles. The centerpiece is made of a couple of white dahlias floating in a bowl.

1 I like the idea of having a pair of tables in the dining room. For a smaller group I can use one, and for a larger group, I simply join the two tables together.

2 The second table in my dining room comes alive with the elongated shapes of sculpture vases stuffed with dahlia blossoms and studded with thick tapers on tall glass candlesticks, which continues the theme of the centerpiece (I believe in working with one theme).

3 For an inexpensive solution for a centerpiece, try these silver balls, pillar candles, and bowls filled to overflowing with fruits.

4 A sheet of lime-green Lucite reinvents my dining table for spring and creates a wonderful contrast with anything I choose to put on it. The centerpiece is a metal basket filled with limes, deep purple eggplant, and purple dendrobium orchids.

1 The kitchen is the heart of my home. It's where I read the paper, prepare my meals, check the occasional e-mail, and plan my day. I thrive on a very functional kitchen and have a great relationship between the oven/refrigerator, cooktop, and sink—known as the "triangle theory," as it creates an ideal relationship for cooking.

2 If only this table could talk! I've shared many a memorable brunch, lunch, or dinner at the dining table in my kitchen. The wall is hand-painted in shades of gray depicting LED screens from the 1950s to today (since, let's face it, all our information nowadays comes to us, in one way or another, on a screen).

3 My everyday basic white collection of china is located directly above the dishwasher for easy packing and unpacking and allows me to reinvent my tabletop by injecting color in the form of glasses, bowls, and chargers (it takes me from drab to fab in an instant!).

4 Even though I live in New York City, I seldom dine in restaurants and prefer to make use of my favorite room in the house—the kitchen—where I entertain friends and family members up to four or five times a week!

5 To keep your silverware neat and tidy, I recommend dividers. These Lucite ones allow you to store several sets of silver, one stacked above the other, in a single drawer.

1 Order, order! I like to know that every single item in my kitchen has a place.

2 In my freezer, I keep a fun collection of different-shaped ice cubes that I pair up with various cocktails (for more about my couture cubes, see page 145).

3 In the laundry room, I keep a second refrigerator and freezer, stocked to the brim with items I don't have space for in my kitchen.

4 To allow me to entertain at a moment's notice or whip up an easy weeknight supper, I keep on hand a dozen organic chickens, racks of lamb, frozen soups, as well as chicken, beef, and veal stock.

5 These sliding doors allow me to seal off the kitchen from the dining area when I'm entertaining. Though for more informal occasions, I keep an "open door" policy!

6 This contemporary gold flatware I designed is like modern jewelry for the table.

7 Multiple sets of flatware allow us to reinvent (and decorate) our tables with style and panache. With today's competitive price points, great-looking flatware is no longer expensive.

8 When spice bottles are arranged alphabetically, with their labels facing out, you can find the cardamom at a moment's notice.

9 Glasses and other cocktail accoutrements for an instant celebration.

10 Keep all bags, foil, and plastic wraps in one handy drawer. Mine fit the way they do by sheer luck!

11 Drawer dividers keep all my utensils well organized.

1. A warm and inviting bed with throws, pillows, and a comforter are key ingredients for a cold winter's night. . . . For added warmth, find an electric blanket or invest in a cashmere-covered hot water bottle.

2. A bunch of delicious tulips placed next to the bed makes for a cheerful awakening in the morning. I also use a three-switch lightbulb so I can control the ambience of the bedroom.

3. There is nothing quite as luxurious as a cool, pristinely ironed bed, with crisp, lightly starched sheets—my favorite summertime indulgence after a hot day on the beach.

4. A cashmere throw at the foot of my summer bed gets me ready for those end-of-summer nights when the temperature drops but I'm not quite ready to bring out the heavy wool guns.

5. In the wintertime months, I'm kept warm by using an electric blanket on top of the mattress, flannel sheets, and a thick warm comforter.

6. The ultimate low-maintenance spring bed. Simply fluff out the duvet in the morning and replace the pillows on top.

7. A high-maintenance bed: This spring bed is made in the hotel style, well tailored, with crisply ironed sheets and linens (believe me, it's well worth the effort).

My jeans stacked neatly and elegantly, department-store style, saving valuable hanging space.

No dressing room or closet is complete without a mirror.

Having a stool or ottoman near or in your dressing room is always helpful when tying your shoes and dressing.

All my shirts are color-coded, from whites to darks, with their collars facing the same way.

Is there any cologne bottle that's not drop-dead beautiful? Display them all on one shelf.

Shoes are arranged from top to bottom, light to dark, toes pointed out, for easy reference.

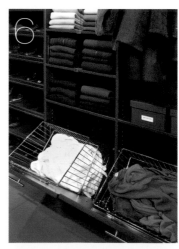

1 As with everything else in my wardrobe, my neckties are divided among solid colors, stripes, polka dots, and every groovy graphic in between!

2 Personal touches: A fresh flower, a photograph of my mother, a couple of objets, and a fragrant candle add just the right touch to my dressing room.

3 Keep your closet well edited. If you buy a new jacket, give away one you no longer wear to someone who could really use it!

4 I use fragrant sticks to keep my dressing room smelling fresh, and the CD player sets the mood when I'm assembling my next outfit.

5 These smaller boxes work well for seasonal shoes.

6 A pair of hampers—one for whites, one for colors—keep the area orderly.

7 These clearly labeled boxes allow me to store specialty travel items, or baseball caps, or seasonal clothing.

8 A top-locked drawer allows me to arrange my valuables, such as watches, rings, sunglasses, and jewelry.

9 My collection of white starched shirts.

10 I even make room for waisted space—in this case, my collection of leather and canvas belts.

11 As I'm not crazy about the reach-in-and-grab philosophy, even my socks and underwear know where they belong!

12 From a sewing kit to a sneaker cleaner, I dedicate one drawer to all the products I need to maintain my wardrobe.

Placemats are stored in large plastic containers for convenience. One shelf is dedicated to candlesticks, another to candle holders, yet another to tapers, columns, and votives.

Champagne
Veuve
Cliquot

My gift closet is filled with beautifully wrapped candles and bottles of Champagne, so I never have to run out the door empty-handed!

candle

candle

candle

1

2

3

1 I keep a couple of comfy chairs in my bedroom. That way, if I can't sleep, or if I have a midnight yen to read, I won't disturb the rest of the house.

2 A chic silk bedspread and a classic arrangement of roses change the mood of the room pictured opposite, above left.

3 A water carafe filled with filtered water instead of a commercial water bottle (which would add a negative impact on the environment). Besides, it looks more chic this way.

4 The guest room is always 100 percent ready to receive guests. Playing hotelier, I sometimes place a floor mat outside the bed, as well as a pair of fresh, cushy slippers.

1 Even if you're sleeping on a sofa bed, it can be just as inviting and welcoming as a regular bed, with crisp, coordinated sheets, a soft blanket, and a comfortable pillow.

2 To make my guests feel comfortable and welcome, the coffee table doubles as a nightstand, with a carafe of ice water, a drinking glass, fresh flowers, an alarm clock, and a good book.

3 When not having guests, my guest room serves as a great media room.

4 Pre-movie cocktails await on a tray.

5 On the sofa bed: the television remote, laminated instructions for TiVo and DVD operation, some Kleenex for those sad movies, licorice and some salty nuts—everything to get you through the movie!

Clockwise from top left: Fresh flowers, fragrant candles, and neatly arranged toiletries make this well-appointed guest bathroom wonderfully welcoming; built on natural colors and textures, the space is both spa-like and inviting; a couple of fresh flowers placed on luxurious towels is a small detail that makes a big impact; use a decorative box and fill it with ointments, lotions, nail clippers, scrubbing brushes, or any other amenity that you feel would make your guests' stay more comfortable. One of my favorite indulgences? Showering outdoors, accessorized with copious towels and quality bathroom products.

1–3 Good lighting is key to any bathroom—and every bathroom should have a dimmer switch (as should every other room in the house!). Placing mouthwash in a wine decanter is much more elegant than leaving it in its commercial container. A large tropical leaf is hardy and has a lot of presence.

4–6 Mirror, mirror, on the wall: a floor-to-ceiling mirror doubles the size of any small bathroom (and reminds you if you're up or down a pound). These Kiehl's hospitality-sized products, which I collect from my travels, come in handy in the guest room. When using linen hand towels, use two wastebaskets, one for garbage and the other for laundry. Place a towel over the laundry bin to indicate to guests which is which.

7–9 A shot of color and a fresh flower add life to the powder room. Accessorize, accessorize, accessorize! Candles, shells, and cachepots complete the picture. These soaps look particularly elegant when placed in a silver candy dish.

10 Make your bathroom experience as over-the-top pleasurable as possible. Start with fluffy, good-quality towels; make sure your iPod's hooked up; spoil yourself with lots of scrubs, rubs, and lotions—and transform your bathroom from an everyday experience to a spa experience!

four

fearless entertaining

So many icons of entertaining have bombarded us with lavish entertaining guides and elaborate cookbooks over the years that many of us have developed entertaining anxiety. We're led to believe that we have to be perfect supermen and superwomen, and create everything from scratch. But in today's hectic, time-starved culture, it is simply not possible, and your best is more than good enough! You should enjoy the process, not dread or suffer through it. A party, no matter how big or how small, is not an audition; it's an occasion to share good times and delicious food with great friends.

Three main misconceptions cause many people to shy away from entertaining:

1. They're afraid it will cost too much money.

2. They're afraid it will take too much time.

3. They're afraid they just don't have the ability.

But the truth is that entertaining has nothing to do with spending large amounts of cash or impressing people. It's about creating memories and moments that your friends and family will cherish. Your guests are there to enjoy being with you, and they're grateful you invited them in the first place!

The secret to elegant entertaining is surprisingly simple: Create a relaxed, friendly atmosphere where you and your guests feel welcome. Order in, set up a buffet, or place the dishes on platters in the center of the table and have your guests serve themselves.

And it all starts with you! If you're a nervous, anxiety-ridden host, you'll end up with nervous, anxiety-ridden guests. But if you set the mood, relax, and enjoy yourself,

your guests will, too. From designing the invitations, to choosing a theme, to preparing for your guests—whether it's a potluck dinner in your kitchen, a buffet in your dining room, or a formal sit-down event for eighteen people—the principles are always the same! Here are a few that have never let me down:

- Avoid being overly ambitious when creating a menu. Choose recipes that allow you to do as much preparation in advance as possible. The idea is to be glued to your dining room chair, not chained to your kitchen stove.

- Start with the best possible ingredients and do as little to them as possible (this cuts down the margin of error). A three-course meal including salad (or other simple appetizer), entrée, and dessert is appropriate for all but the most skilled entertainer.

It's also irrelevant who makes the food and where it comes from. Serve take-out food, prepurchased gourmet food, or drop off a casserole dish at your favorite restaurant and have them prepare a stew that you can reheat while you toss a store-bought salad. My mantra is, If the baker down the road makes a better tart than you do, then by all means purchase his! One day, while sampling a Chicken Tikka Masala and a Basmati Rice from the supermarket, I said to myself, *This is amazing, there's no way I can improve on it.* So that night I brought home several premade containers of it and prepared my own side dishes to accompany them. The meal was a great success, not to mention incredibly easy. Here's the bottom line: Today's supermarkets and gourmet delis offer some excellent ready-made soups, prewashed salads, tasty side dishes, and mouthwatering entrées.

- If you decide to cook the entire meal, choose a foolproof menu. Avoid soufflés and sauces that will collapse or curdle if you're fifteen minutes off schedule because your guests are enjoying one another over cocktails, or someone is running late. Savory stews, soups, and casseroles are wonderful because they can be prepared (in large part) ahead of time.

- Food is like theater, and first impressions count for everything—so make the first course simple but spectacular. If your meal begins with a bland brown soup, the performance can only go downhill from there! Choose a dish that is visual as well as delicious and that balances color, temperature, texture, and taste. By adding chopped chives to the brown soup along with a dollop of nonfat yogurt, or serving a salad of baby greens with grilled prawns, chopped mint, and feta cheese, you set the tone for a wildly colorful evening. The idea is to appeal to all the senses and make your dishes exciting. By adding vivid garnishes, you layer flavors and textures, which is the best way to add your touch to store-bought dishes—or your own!

- Allow twenty to thirty minutes per course. My dinner parties usually end at the table, unless someone wants to smoke cigarettes or cigars, in which case we adjourn to another room to continue talking or to smoke after I've served dessert and coffee.

Special Occasions: Planning Makes All the Difference

Be Our Guest: Invitations

An invitation to an informal occasion is easy: Give someone a call, a fax with fun graphics, an e-mail with a picture attached. Fill in a preprinted card or make something yourself. Home computers and printers can accommodate most card stock and vellum, allowing you maximum artistic freedom! The level of informality of the occasion you have in mind will dictate what's right. You're not throwing an inaugural ball, so do what's easy and have fun with it.

For more formal occasions, a professionally printed invitation sets the stage for what's to come. It lets your guests know whether the gathering calls for business attire or black tie, whether it's cocktails only or dinner and dancing. The color scheme, font, and paper can be simple or elaborate. There are no set rules, so by all means, let your imagination be your guide.

- Weave a thread of style throughout the celebration, starting with the invitation and ending with dessert. If you've selected a distinct color scheme for the celebration, match the invitations to your party decorations. The ink color, envelope lining, and card stock can be the same color or within the same color family as you'll be using in your table setting. For example, if you're wild about green, go all out! Try celadon ink on white or ecru stock, white ink on green stock, a centerpiece of green apples and limes, forest-green napkins tied with a chartreuse ribbon, and as a finale to your dinner, green tea ice cream!

- If the beach is your thing, attach a shell to the invitation, stencil a silhouette of an oyster on the menu, and write guests' names on conches in lieu of place cards! Be kitsch if kitsch feels right—or keep things elegant and restrained with a few hints of your theme here and there!

Suggestion: When writing an invitation to an unmarried couple, gay or straight, one half of whom is better known to you, always include the other partner by name on the envelope and in the letter. If you can't recall the other person's name, take the trouble to call a mutual acquaintance who does before sending the note.

- Here's another idea for a great invitation: Give your guests written instructions regarding their look for the night. A note to "Wear something red," spices things up right from the start and gives everyone a great excuse to go shopping for something in scarlet!

Dream Up a Theme

You've invited friends to your home for breakfast, brunch, cocktails, dinner, or coffee and dessert. So why not create a distinctive theme for your get-together?

- Thanks to Oprah, book clubs are everywhere. Elevate the conversation with food plotted thematically around the novel or memoir du jour. Discussing *The Grapes of Wrath* will be a lot more interesting when you serve wine made from California grapes.

- Invite friends over for a scotch-tasting in the winter, with each couple bringing a single-malt scotch. Serve a savory stew on a nest of pasta or a tangy rice dish.

- Invite friends to a Champagne tasting, with each guest bringing their favorite chocolates, or splurge with two ounces of caviar and enjoy a favorite bottle of bubbly.

- Host a potluck dinner, assigning everyone a different course. Nothing could be easier, and explaining each dish serves as an instant icebreaker.

- Spend an evening in Morocco by serving a fabulous Chicken Tagine over couscous and screening *Casablanca*. Or take everyone on a trip to Spain with paella and the latest Pedro Almodóvar offering. Or invite friends for a grand marnier soufflé and pop a Gerard Depardieu movie into your DVD player—that way you and your guests will always have Paris!

The Sky Is the Limit, from Lunch to Late-Night Dessert

There are countless ways to entertain. Surrounded by great friends, in your kitchen, with the food coming straight out of the oven and onto plates. Or more formally, at a sit-down birthday celebration for twenty-four. Or any of several memorable variations in between. Here are some starting points for your own inspiring meals:

A Simple Lunch
When: 12:30 P.M.
What: An easy, delicious midday feast with one or two great friends, either for business, pleasure, or something in between.

Quick and Easy Lunch Buffet
When: 1:00 P.M.
What: A wonderfully casual way to bring friends together (some who may not know one another) and mingle while sampling a wide showcase of tasty foods. Try to balance your buffet selection with a protein, a carb, vegetables, and grains! Cardinal rule: *Never* put fish and meat on the same buffet table. Surf and turf don't work. If God wanted us to have surf and turf, he would have given cows claws and lobsters hooves! For more on setting a buffet, see page 163.

Afternoon Tea (not to be confused with High Tea, below)
When: 3:00 or 3:30 P.M.
What: The Duchess of Bedford came up with this little treat to stave off hunger pangs between lunch and dinner.
Food: Elegant pastries, crumpets, scones, madeleines, finger sandwiches. Buy or bake a batch of scones to serve with clotted cream and preserves; or buy decadent cakes, tarts, and cookies from your favorite bakery.

High Tea
When: 5:00 P.M.
What: Originally created to satisfy English workers after a long day of labor, this is perfect if you're meeting for a post-theater-matinee dinner.
Food: Hearty tea served in a mug with heavier fare such as a Welsh rarebit or a stew of lamb or poultry.

The Cocktail Party: Come for Drinks!
When: Cocktail parties generally take place from 6:00 to 8:00 P.M. or 6:00 to 9:00 P.M.
What: A cocktail party is one of my favorite occasions—wonderfully old-fashioned, but with a modern update! To plan one, all you need are equal quantities of snappy cocktails, delicious food, groovy music, and colorful people. See page 141 for much more on cocktail parties.

The Dinner Party (my favorite activity of the day!)

When: 8:00 P.M. or later. Seat guests at the table between 8:45 and 9:00 P.M., after the cocktail hour, which is just that: one hour! Begin to seat people forty-five minutes after the first guests have arrived, which allows fifteen minutes for everyone to get settled.

What: At least a three-course meal, including dessert. The simpler the better. Use the best ingredients and do as little to them as possible. See page 154 for more information on throwing a dinner party.

Late-Night Dessert

When: after 10:00 P.M.

What: Prepare a steaming pot of coffee, light some candles, and bring out a tray with four chocolate pots de crème from the refrigerator. Set up a bottle of dessert wine in an ice bucket, and you are set to go. Finish off with a snifter of Cognac and a cigar. Never too late to keep it chic!

Party Basics

Whether you hire a caterer or not, if you are having twenty-four or more guests, keep in mind that hors d'oeuvres should be bite-sized and passed on trays (by you or a waiter) or set out on a table for guests to help themselves. If foods are on skewers or toothpicks, make sure that someone collects them or that there is a receptacle for them. One easy idea is to cut a lemon in half and place it by the food so that guests can stick the used skewers or toothpicks in it. Avoid tomato- or turmeric-based dipping sauces if you're concerned about your furniture. Keep those recipes for outdoors in the summer.

Here are a few great ideas:

- For a group of twenty-four or more: Set up several different stations in and around the living room, pairing food types with appropriate wines and beverages. Pair a green and white platter of crudités (raw vegetables) on the coffee table with a sauvignon blanc, or set out a selection of cheeses and dried and candied fruit paired with vintage port on the dining table. For something heartier, offer a platter of assorted grilled sausages with a selection of mustards, and give guests their choice of a variety of mismatched red wines from your cellar on a sideboard; dazzle them with smoked salmon or gravlax with frozen vodka or aquavit on another table. Serve coffee, chocolates, and biscotti in the den. This ensures that the guests will circulate and enjoy a gastronomic experience without needing so much service. The tables, linens, and flatware for the stations or vignettes can be set up the day before.

- For a cocktail reception, prepare small soups by serving store-bought gazpacho with a lump of crabmeat in a demitasse cup. In the fall or early winter, serve small coffee cups of risotto with shaved truffles or a big asparagus risotto casserole. Risotto is both chic and a little more substantial. Beef it up by passing medallions of New York steak served on bamboo skewers with Dijon mustard sauce. Add decadence with some butter-mashed potatoes.

"My formula for successful entertaining? Snappy cocktails, tasty food, groovy music, and colorful people—in equal quantities!"

fearless entertaining

- Always keep a couple dozen frozen puff pastry sausage rolls or samosas in the freezer for last-minute or unexpected cocktails. (See pages 38–45 for more pantry and kitchen essentials that will keep you prepared for drop-bys.)

- Serve small dumplings on Chinese soup spoons or a scoop of tuna tartare on dinner spoons.

- For dessert, you'll score big points for serving crème brûlée, or chocolate pots de crème, or tropical fruit salad with coconut sorbet in espresso cups. Really pressed for resources? Serve coffee with biscotti and some chocolate truffles. Frozen, ready-to-bake chocolate chip cookie dough is another fantastic option for a last-minute flourish.

- As for music, the first choice and the easiest is a fabulous playlist of your favorite foot-tapping music from any genre. You need energetic music or upbeat jazz at a cocktail party.

Cocktail Party Basics

The Missing Clink

There is nothing quite like a well-crafted, wonderfully garnished concoction in the right glass to make your guests feel welcome or to jump-start a soiree. And one of the biggest trends I see today is the triumphant return of the cocktail. Fresh, bold, colorful, sexy variations on classic cocktails such as ice-cold martinis, apple sours, and cosmopolitans—served chilled and garnished in a gorgeous glass—are a nod to the glamour of the past, enlivened with a sexy new twist. As a devotee of all things chic and elegant, I couldn't be more thrilled.

Most cocktails are quite potent, and a good stiff drink is all but guaranteed to rev up any party. When you're serving a tray of Manhattans in the dead of winter, or Chili Passion Martinis midsummer, you'll be surprised how often guests opt for the cocktail over the habitual choice of red or white! Wine and beer are fine, but consider offering your guests a signature drink instead; they'll appreciate the thought and enjoy trying something different.

For added style, moisten the rim and frost your cocktail glasses with a variety of delicious, colorful concoctions. Shaved chocolate, ground espresso, and flavored sugar can add just the right flavor. Liquor stores offer countless premixed blends and cocktail concoctions as well as garnishing options that taste absolutely delicious. Some of my favorites are from a company called Stirrings. I love their Lemon Drop and Tangerini martini mixes. (See the sidebar at right for directions on how to rim a glass.)

A delicious cocktail should be only a fingertip away (see my recommendations for a well-stocked bar on pages 45 and 46). Keep all cocktail essentials and your hard liquor on a shelf in a closet, or a cabinet in the dining room, or in your kitchen cupboard, or even in your living room armoire. Set it up before guests arrive so it's ready and waiting. Inside, arrange your glasses along with an ice bucket, cocktail napkins, and a selection of liquors, stirrers, stoppers, and mixers.

A Special Treat

Rimming the glass of your cocktail has become all the rage. Try it with colored sugars, shaved chocolate, ground espresso, or carmelized sugar. Champagne glasses, rocks glasses, and even double old fashioned glasses work perfectly. If you're using a dry blend, wet the rim of the glass with a lemon or orange peel, then carefully dip the rim of the glass into your coating. Twirl the glass around as you remove it to make sure the rim is coated evenly.

Here are some of my favorite libations, which have made many of my parties a hit—and inspired much pleasure and many memories along the way.

cocktail #1
Chili Passion

Friends of mine own the Setai Hotel in Miami. I tasted this fantastic drink there. It's alive with flavor and sweet and spicy on the palette. Definitely one of my favorite drinks!

- 1 ounce cranberry juice
- 1 ounce orange juice
- 2 ounces Captain Morgan's Parrot Bay Passion Fruit Rum
- 1 ounce passion fruit puree
- ¼ ounce fresh ginger juice (½ cup ginger per two cups of water, brewed slowly—do not boil—for fifteen to twenty minutes)
- 8 to 12 seeds of red Thai chili pepper, 3 to 4 pieces of chopped-up chili, and 1 red Thai chili pepper, sliced, for garnish (slice it so it adheres to the glass!) Nutmeg for garnish

Combine all of the juices, puree, rum, and the chili pepper seeds and chopped-up chili. Add to a cocktail shaker two thirds full of ice. Shake for fifteen seconds, strain, and pour into a martini glass. Garnish with the sliced red chili pepper by attaching it to the rim of the glass, or simply float the chili in the drink. *Do not* eat the chili! Top with a dash of nutmeg.

cocktail #2
Lemon Drop

- ¼ ounce fresh lemon juice
- ½ ounce Cointreau or triple sec
- 2 ounces citrus vodka
  Sugar, for rimming the glass
- 1 lemon wheel, for garnish

Chill the martini glasses in the freezer until frosted (another option: place crushed ice in the glass, swirl, and discard the ice). Wet the rim of the glass with part of the lemon, and press it into a saucer of sugar to rim the glass. Shake the lemon juice, Cointreau, and vodka in a shaker two thirds full of ice, and strain into the glass. Float a thin wheel of lemon on top of the drink.

To serve as a shooter, follow the recipe above but strain into three one-ounce shot glasses. Cover the mouth of the glass with a sugar-dusted wheel of lemon.

cocktail #3
Raspberry and Elderflower Champagne Cocktail

As an alternative to a glass of "pure" Champagne, this elegant drink will surprise your tongue with its mix of flavors.

- ¼ shot Chambord
- ¼ shot elderflower cordial, available at most liquor stores
  Chilled Champagne

Add the Chambord and cordial to a Champagne flute and top with Champagne.

cocktail #4
Strepe Chepe
(One of my best friends, Sloan Lindemann, created this cocktail and gave it its wonderfully nonsensical name!)

One of my all-time favorite party drinks. I love serving them in test tubes or shot glasses, set in an ice block. In addition to being thirst quenching, they are guaranteed to make any party blast off!

- 1   cup vodka (8 ounces)
- 2   tablespoons fresh lime juice
- 3   tablespoons fine sugar, plus additional to taste
- ½   cup packed mint leaves
- 2   cups ice cubes

Add all ingredients to the blender. Blend until smooth and uniform. Add additional sugar to taste. Serve in Champagne flutes or shot glasses.

cocktail #5
Vodka-Espresso Shot

When it's time to party, tray-pass a few of these in sexy martini glasses or shot glasses. Turn the music up and prepare for a good time—the caffeine and alcohol do the trick! For a twist, try substituting tequila for vodka. (My favorite is Don Julio 1942.) But remember rule 101 of cocktails: If you start the night with tequila, *end* the night with tequila. Mixing liquors is a hangover looking for a head to call its home.

- 1   ounce premium vodka or tequila
- ½   ounce Kahlua Especial (70 proof)
- ½   ounce Tia Maria
- 1   ounce cold espresso
- 1   orange peel
- 1   teaspoon chocolate powder, for rimming the glass
- 1   pinch red chili pepper, for rimming the glass

Prepare shot glasses or a martini glass by rimming the top with an orange peel. On a saucer, mix the chocolate powder and the red chili pepper, and press the rim of the glass into the mixture. Combine the vodka or tequila, Kahlua, Tia Maria, and cold espresso in a shaker filled with ice; then shake, strain, and pour.

cocktail #6
Sgroppino

Sgroppino is a fashionable after-dinner drink that can double as dessert. In Venice it's made with vodka, top-quality lemon sorbet, and the dry Venetian sparkling wine Prosecco.

- 5 to 6 tablespoons of lemon sorbet
- 1   tablespoon vodka (or grappa)
- 2   tablespoons Prosecco, chilled

Mix all ingredients in a blender for thirty seconds until creamy and thick. Serve immediately in a Champagne flute.

A Scotch Primer

Scotch is ideal for certain occasions: when the first nip of fall is in the air; when friends are sitting around a crackling fire in midwinter; or simply as an earthy, smoky, sweater-wearing alternative to vodka, gin, and tequila.

Here's what you need to know about this British Isles superstar:

- If you want the best scotch, always go for the single malt! Single malts come from a single distillery, and they are not blended with other whiskeys.

- A reliable rule of thumb is that the longer the scotch has been aged in barrels, the smoother it will taste going down. A truly amazing-tasting scotch will have been aged for at least ten years. Twelve-, fifteen-, and twenty-one-year-old scotches are available (and incomparable!), but they are also much higher priced. Make sure that when you buy single malt, you know how old it is!

- Scotch is usually served neat (without mixers) at room temperature. Many people like it over large rocks or sometimes with a splash of soda. The bigger the ice cube, the colder the cocktail, and the slower the melt ratio.

- Like wine, scotch should be stored in a dark, slightly cool location, placed on its side or standing upright.

Tequila 101

I love tequila. It's my Friday-evening cocktail for the simple reasons that unlike most spirits, tequila is an upper rather than a downer and it works quickly! A well-crafted tequila is clean, delicious, and goes down as smooth as silk. When many of us think of tequila, we have flashbacks to college days and a drink that tasted like carburetor cleaner or paint stripper and gave us a hangover to match. For twenty years I believed that, too, but the tequilas of today match some of the world's great vodkas and Cognacs in taste and quality.

My absolute favorite is Don Julio 1942, which has hints of apple in the nose and a smooth, sweet taste with notes of vanilla in the finish. It can be stored in the freezer, and when you're ready to dive in, consider forgoing margaritas or sunrise cocktails and serving it on the rocks in a Champagne glass with a hint of lime. It's like a fine Cognac, only smoother!

Gin Coherence

Gin is a distillation of white grain spirit and juniper berries. I consider gin a wonderful daytime drink. Few things could be chicer than gin and tonic over ice with a dash of Angostura bitters!

I Vant Some Vodka

Voda in Russian means "water," and with the addition of a *k* the word roughly translates into "little water," though anyone who's had a vodka tonic knows there's a lot more going on in that glass than plain water! In Eastern Europe, people drink vodka in shots, along with food. In America, vodka is typically mixed with sweet syrups, or tonics, and sipped on ice, though I love it with any kind of fresh juice!

Mere Alcohol Doesn't Thrill You at All? Treats for Abstainers

Always have something available for tee-totalers. You can make a simple beverage and embellish it by pouring it into an elegant glass or adding a garnish, whether it's a sprig of mint, a slice of lemon, olives, cocktail onions, maraschino cherries, or a rim of sugar, salt, or powdered chocolate. A nonalcoholic cocktail should be crafted and served with the same care and dedication as a regular cocktail!

A Wine Primer

Whether it's a rich red or a dry, chilled white, wine is one of life's great pleasures. Each is a mystery, and until it's uncorked you never know exactly what's inside.

Here is a list of some of my favorite wines and some of their most outstanding characteristics.

Whites

Chardonnay

The most popular, high-quality white wine, with a luscious, dark golden color and a nutty, fruity, faintly smoky fragrance and taste. Among the most popular brands of French Chardonnays, I like Montrachet, Chablis, and Pouilly-Fouissé, I recom-

Designer Rocks: Fancy Ice Cubes

If you really want to amaze and bedazzle your guests, make your own "couture" ice cubes: star shapes, jewels, and flowers for mixed drinks; long, sexy cylinders for vodka and tequila; and oversized ice wedges for scotch. Setting a great bottle of wine in an ice bucket with jewel-shaped ice next to a pair of sparkling glasses and a bowl of salted nuts is easy to pull together in an instant and very impressive looking!

For mixed drinks, I can tailor the ice cube specifically to whatever drink I'm creating. Example: I'll use a single large ice cube for a scotch on the rocks or a gin and tonic. The large cube is denser, so it has a dramatically slower rate of melting, which keeps the drink icy cold rather than quickly watering it down; or I'll use long, thin icicle-shaped ice that matches up fantastically with tequila or vodka served in a tall, slender glass. The watering down of the drink doesn't lessen its flavor or intensity.

Whenever I see ice trays designed in interesting shapes (often originally intended for children's lollipops or three-dimensional star-shaped cookies), I instead use them for my couture ice cubes. When they're frozen, I place them in Ziploc bags or a small plastic box inside my freezer to keep them from shattering. In the steamy summer months, I'll add fresh fruit to the tray such as red cherries, raspberries, blueberries, blackberries, and green grapes. When the cubes are placed inside summery cocktails, they give an ordinary drink a complete drab-to-fab makeover!

colin cowie chic

mend serving them with seafood, chicken, and pork because the light flavor won't overpower the foods.

Sauvignon Blanc
My favorite white wine, bar none. The grapes that make up a sauvignon blanc are dryer and sharper tasting than Chardonnay grapes, with a grassy, herbaceous aroma and flavor. I typically serve a sauvignon blanc with a starter such as a fresh salad. It also pairs well as an accompaniment to seafood. I prefer to serve this during the day, because it's lighter than a more full-bodied Chardonnay.

Riesling
A native of Germany, the riesling grape also thrives in the cool climates of the eastern United States. While riesling grapes can also produce dry wines, they are best known for their intensely sweet, sophisticated fragrance and taste. They pair particularly well with Asian and fusion foods and can offset their spiciness.

Pinot Grigio
This Italian superstar is crisp and dry on the tongue as well as faintly citrusy. I tend to serve pinot gris and pinot grigio (though the grapes are the same, a pinot gris is fruitier and somewhat less crisp tasting than the latter) anytime I am looking for something on the lighter side!

Reds

Cabernet Sauvignon
The primary grape of Bordeaux, and the basis for most of California's red wines, the complex, fruity cabernet sauvignon is the most popular top-quality red wine. I serve it with meat, game, or before dinner, side by side with a tray of cheeses, or I sometimes have a glass when I get home at the end of the day.

Merlot
Though dryer and smoother, the merlot grape is similar to the cabernet sauvignon in fragrance and taste. It's among the

Wine Storage Basics

If you are planning on investing in fine wines or building a collection, I recommend keeping your bottles under optimal storage conditions. Here are a few things to consider when collecting wines and starting your own cellar.

- Store your wine in a clean, dark, slightly moist location where (if possible) the temperature never varies, as any kind of radical fluctuation in temperature can damage or prematurely age a fine wine. White wines are more prone to spoilage due to varying temperatures than reds. Not all wines should be aged, either. A light, fruity French Beaujolais nouveau should be drunk within days! Sauvignon blancs and light Chardonnays don't require much aging, but a good white Burgundy can benefit from anywhere from three to seven years in storage. And dessert wines, such as Sauternes, get even better over an extremely long time (up to forty years or more).

- The ideal temperature for storing wines is 50 to 55 degrees Fahrenheit, but any temperature between 40 and 65 degrees Fahrenheit works well. Controlling humidity is also important. If your wine cellar isn't humid enough—and optimally, it should be 50 percent—consider buying a humidifier so the corks in the bottles won't dry out. Too much humidity won't affect the wine, but the label may mold!

- Darkness is ideal for a cellar. Light can prematurely age a bottle of wine, and ultraviolet rays are able to penetrate even dark glass, which can lead to a sour, acid fragrance and taste. Sparkling wines and Champagnes are even more sensitive to light than wines, so be extra sure these, too, are kept in optimally unlit conditions, and as far away from the room's source of light as possible (see page 151 for more on Champagne).

- Store wine horizontally so that the liquid stays in contact with the cork. This keeps the cork moist and prevents air from entering the bottle. Once a wine is in place in a wine rack, or anywhere else lying securely on its side, you shouldn't disturb it until you're ready to drink it.

most popular wines in America and softer and less dark than the cabernet. Try a glass with any kind of meat or game.

Beaujolais

A fruity wine, light and dry, Beaujolais nouveau is a new wine, bottled right after fermentation without aging, and should be drunk chilled within a few months' time—and it's also delicious in the summertime with sliced peaches in a tall glass.

Pinot Noir

The primary red grape of Burgundy. Young pinot noirs have the simple fruitiness of cherries, plums, raspberries, and strawberries. More mature ones are smokier. I serve pinot noir with chicken or a fish with a cream sauce, though I never serve it with hot, spicy food because it's not strong enough to stand up against intense flavors.

Zinfandel

California vintners claim the versatile zinfandel as their very own. Spicy and rich or light and fruity, it goes well with just about anything, especially turkey. I also recommend serving it with tomato-based dishes, and with anything containing lots of garlic.

Shiraz

Originating in France's Rhône region, the fruity, peppery Shiraz grape has enormous flavor, and combines to create such renowned labels as Châteauneuf-du-Pape and Côtes-du-Rhône. Shiraz goes exceptionally well with chicken, or even better, duck. Shiraz is also the oldest grape variety known to man, dating back to the Bible!

Sauternes

Sauternes is a rich, sweet dessert wine produced in France's Bordeaux region. The most fabulous is Château d'Yquem (best years: 1976, 1995, and even 2003). I also enjoy the South African Vin de Constance, which was one of Napoléon's favorite dessert wines. Served well chilled, it enhances dessert or even a cheese course.

Serving with Distinction

- White wine is generally served with white meat, including poultry and pork, fish and crustaceans, while red meat is usually paired with a red wine. Serve port or red wine with cheese, sweet wines with dessert, Champagne with caviar or shellfish, frozen vodka or aquavit with smoked salmon or gravlax. But fortunately, today's rules are not set in stone. If you are serving a "white" food with a rich, heavy bordelaise sauce, it might go better with a red pinot noir. Or try out something daring and untested, such as pairing an icy glass of sake with a cold soup.

- As a general rule of thumb, I serve sauvignon blanc with lunch because of its wonderful lightness. I bring out the Chardonnay once the sun has set. I'll drink rose—or for that matter, anything pink!—all summer long, from Memorial Day to Labor Day. I am a huge fan of South African and Australian wines, which are highly drinkable and reasonably priced. I love rieslings and pinot gris, which come from harder, dryer climates in the northern part of France and Germany. They're sophisticated, effervescent, and light on the palate. I also never make the distinction between a cooking wine and a drinking wine. Why cook with a wine you wouldn't also want to drink?

- When I serve white wines, I usually start with the driest wine and work my way toward the sweetest one. With red wines, I start with the lightest wine and move toward the most full-bodied.

- I never recommend pouring wine all the way to the top of the glass. It's more elegant to fill a glass two-thirds full. Stemmed glasses are typically used for both reds and whites. Holding reds by the bowl warms the wine slightly, allowing it to breathe, whereas holding white wines by the stem is appropriate so your body heat doesn't affect the cool temperature. One of today's trends is to drink wine from tumblers, Italian style, rather than in traditional, long-stemmed wine glasses. While I like drinking red this way, I still prefer my whites in a stemmed glass.

Why Decant?: Ripe and Ready

A red-wine bottle should be opened anywhere from twenty minutes to two hours before you take your first sip (white wines are usually not decanted). The reason for this is grounded in simple science. You are maximizing the wine's exposure to the air in the room, allowing it to breathe and warm up, and its flavors to blossom and mellow.

If you don't decant your wine, most wines will still improve noticeably if you uncork them twenty minutes before your guests arrive. If the wine is of a recent vintage, it will open up far more quickly than an older wine (the one time in life when youth isn't all that beneficial!), because younger wines have already been aged in the barrel and are ready to be drunk. Lighter-bodied wines, such as pinot noir, which have lower tannin levels, need little if any time to breathe. But with older wines, which have more than their fair share of tannin, decanting is an absolute necessity.

You can use any glass pourer for a decanter, so long as it has a wide enough opening on the top (anywhere from two to four inches) for the wine to breathe properly. If you don't own an actual decanter, you can use a glass pitcher, or even a glass flower vase if you can pour safely from it. Or pour your wine into glasses you've set out on a tray about twenty minutes before you serve it, and let nature take its course. The wine will open wonderfully.

When seasoned wine drinkers open a bottle of wine, they invariably sniff the cork. They're simply gathering more information about the wine. Has the wine been in contact with the cork? Good. Does the cork have a moldy or vinegary smell? Not good, as this means that the wine has oxidized and turned sour. Sometimes you'll find crystals resembling salt adhering to the cork, which are simply tartaric acid, a naturally occurring, harmless substance from the grapes.

If a wine has gone bad, it will have a noticeably sharp and unpleasant odor, like ammonia. In the case of white wines, you will often know if a wine has turned just by a simple glance (an oxidized white wine has turned an unsightly brown color). Before drinking, do as the experts do: First sniff the wine. Now swirl a small amount of wine in your glass and sniff again to note if the bouquet has changed at all. Take a small sip before drinking. This releases more of the wine's fragrances, and also allows you to visually examine the wine. Is it at all cloudy or discolored? It shouldn't be, unless you are drinking an unfiltered wine.

The Elegant Extra: Champagne Explained

To me, Champagne will always be the ne plus ultra of all alcoholic confections. It's the beverage most associated with celebration and memorable moments. It has captivated me as an expression of pure glamour, unparalleled sophistication, and bliss ever since I first spied James Bond extracting a chilled bottle of 1988 Bollinger Grand Année Champagne from a secret compartment in his Aston Martin.

True Champagne must come from France's Champagne region, located ninety or so miles northeast of Paris. Those other white, often wonderful, kinds of bubbly are sparkling, or effervescent, wines (the term for "sparkling" is *spumante* in Italy, *sekt* in German, and *cava* in Spain). Many of the best-known Champagne houses, including Moët & Chandon, Roederer, and Taittinger, have all opened up vineyards in California, and they produce excellent-quality sparkling wines. The homegrown results can be delicious, but it's still not Champagne!

Generally speaking, the finest-tasting and most expensive Champagne is vintage Champagne. Vintage Champagnes are at their very best—and most complex—anywhere from eight to fifteen years of age. Nonvintage Champagnes will noticeably improve in aroma and taste in five years' time, which isn't to say a freshly opened bottle of nonvintage Bollinger still won't knock your socks off! Champagnes range from light to full-bodied. For an exceptional light Champagne, I like Taittinger or Perrier-Jouët; for medium body, I suggest Moët & Chandon (producers of Dom Pérignon); and for a complex, full-bodied Champagne, my favorites include Veuve Clicquot, Krug, Dom Pérignon, Louis Roederer Cristal, and also Bollinger Grande Année—in tribute to my favorite Aston Martin–driving man of action.

- Look on the label of your Champagne for the words *Champagne, France,* and the word *brut,* which means that the Champagne is dry. If your taste runs to less dry Champagnes, the word *demi-sec* will steer you in the right direction. A demi-sec is usually served with dessert. Veuve Clicquot makes a great demi-sec; it's ideal for weddings because, like the bride, it's dressed in white!

- Champagne is best well chilled! I always keep a couple bottles in my refrigerator. If you need to chill it quickly, place it in the freezer for forty minutes (set a kitchen timer!), or place the bottle in an ice bucket with plenty of ice. Add some water to the bucket so the base of the bottle is covered by about two inches, and let chill for at least thirty minutes, or longer if you can.

- Avoid popping a Champagne cork! With that much pressure bottled up, a flying cork could easily cause an accident. It's safer and more elegant to remove the cork slowly and gradually. Keep your hands on the cork so it doesn't pop after the wire is removed. (They say the sound when opening a bottle of Champagne should be like the sigh of a satisfied woman . . .)

- Champagne is best served in glass or crystal Champagne flutes. The tall and lean shape of the flute keeps the seductive bubbles from escaping. To serve, pour the Champagne in small amounts in several flutes at once, then top each off as the foamy bubbles subside. You may have to do this three or four times to fill the flutes two-thirds full.

- Cheers!

A Port Primer

A glass of mature, sweet, and flavorful vintage port from Portugal is a great ending to any dinner. Served in small glasses, it makes a wonderfully chic addition to a cheese course, before dessert, or simply on its own. It also pairs beautifully with foie gras in the winter.

There are infinite types of port wine, but the two finest are vintage ports and tawny ports.

- Vintage ports are the most exceptional and often among the highest priced. The most acclaimed vintages of this half century were, in order of year, not quality: 1955, 1963, 1970, 1977, 1983, 1985, and 1992.

- Tawny ports come from a blend of grapes from several different years, and are wood aged for fifty years or longer.

- The most renowned port producer of vintage and tawny ports are Cockburn's, Croft, Dow's, Fonseca, Graham's, Quinta do Noval, Sandeman, Taylor Fladgate, and Warre's.

- Store port on its side, but twenty-four hours before serving, stand the port bottle upright, allowing the sediment to settle on the bottom. When it's time to serve, chill the port by placing it in the refrigerator for thirty minutes; carefully remove the cork, then decant the port into another container to separate the wine from its sediment. Serve at once. Both wood-aged and bottled-aged port wines are generally served at cool room temperatures (64 to 68 degrees Fahrenheit).

- Traditional port glasses are smaller than wineglasses.

- Recork the port bottle immediately after serving and store in a cool place. Vintage ports should be consumed within twenty-four hours of opening the bottle, but aged tawny ports can last up to a month after decanting.

A Few Other Delicacies

Cognac

Unlike ports, which are classified by year, Cognac is a brandy distilled from white wine and produced in and around Cognac, France. Vintners classify Cognac by name: VS (Very Special, famous for its golden yellow color); VSOP (Very Special Old Pale, which is subtle, spicy, and regal tasting); and XO (Extraordinary Reserve, which is rich and incomparably full-bodied). My absolute favorite Cognacs are Hine or Rémy Martin Louis XIII, which I typically serve after dessert.

Armagnac

Armagnac is a rich, concentrated distilled French grape brandy and *not,* as is sometimes believed, a brand of Cognac! Often aged for twenty years or longer, it's full-flavored and goes down smoothly. Enjoy only vintage, or *hors d'âge,* which means only that it's "beyond age," or simply, that its age is too old to determine!

Other Fantastic Digestifs

They include Grand Marnier, Amaretto, brandy, Cointreau, Drambuie, kirsch, and crème de cassis.

Time to Chill

It's been a long day. You've spent most of it returning e-mails, making calls, and running meetings, seminars, errands, and yourself absolutely ragged! The time has come to let go of work, enjoy a little downtime, and recharge.

Transforming the mood and energy of a house from A.M. chaos to P.M. mellow is the first step toward reconnecting with yourself. Getting back to your more relaxed self is the first step toward reconnecting with the people you love.

To make the shift from hectic to heavenly, appeal to all five senses. Turn down the lamps, light a candle in the bathroom, fix a drink, change your clothes and your shoes, and put on some music! Turn up the beat if you're ready to have fun; wind it down if you're looking to chill.

A few other great ways to go from A.M. to P.M.:

- On the weekends, after exercising, I take a steam, followed by a relaxing bath. Soaking in the hot water, I can feel the stress draining out of my body, and I begin to relax and recharge.

- Sitting down to read a book is a true luxury. I love reading, and consider it one of the great relaxers of all time. I always have three or four books on my reading list at all times. (Whenever I read something I love, whether it's fiction, memoir, history, or poetry, I'll buy five or six copies and share them with friends. I get great pleasure from sharing the written word.)

Humidors and Hollywood: A Cigar Primer

Few things conjure up an image of Hollywood glamour (or look more elegant) than a well-dressed gentleman or lady smoking a cigar. Cigars are distinguished by their brand, color, shape, size, and most important, their taste. Cuba is to cigars what Champagne is to sparkling wine. Cuba used to make the world's most magnificent cigars, which haven't been available in the United States for nearly fifty years. Here's what you need to know.

- Brand: The cigar brands I recommend include Arturo Fuente, Ashton, Davidoff, Macanudo, Montecristo, Partagas, and Punch.

- Color: Lighter-colored cigars usually taste milder than darker ones, though there are exceptions. A better indication of a cigar's taste and potency is its country of origin. I tend to reserve my cigar smoking for when I'm visiting Europe, at which point I'm irresistibly drawn to Cuban cigars!

- Shape: Cigars are either *parejos,* which are linear and straight-sided, or *figurados,* which are known for their atypical shapes, such as torpedoes and even pyramids.

- Storage: A humidor is a special box that keeps cigars at an optimum temperature and humidity. A humidor should maintain a consistently tropical environment between 68 and 70 degrees Fahrenheit. If you don't have a humidor, store cigars in a box, but make sure it's airtight. Place a damp sponge or towel in the box to keep the tobacco moist, but the cigars should be protected from actual contact. When traveling, you can pack them in a plain old Ziploc bag.

The Daily De-Stress

Today I made my way into my office at 6:00 A.M., my cell and landline phones began ringing, 187 overnight e-mails and half a dozen phone messages greeted me. Over the next ten hours, I tended to approximately one hundred more calls, e-mails, interruptions, and small and major crises, all of which conspired to create one of the most exhausting days in memory.

Days such as this are part and parcel of running a successful business and of everyday life. After a twelve-hour period like this, replenishing oneself isn't a frivolity; it becomes a necessity. Even on an uneventful day (which frankly isn't very common for me), I take at least an hour to restore my balance, serenity, and energy. I highly recommend you do, too. Otherwise you will feel like all you've done all day is give out to others—your lover, family, friends, and coworkers. Those sixty minutes become your reward in recognition of your energy and spirit, and I promise you will feel—as I do—rejuvenated afterward.

The best way I know to begin my day on a stress-free note is to exercise first thing in the morning. If for some reason that's not possible, I will still do *something* athletic. For more ways to de-stress, see page 153.

- Or what about a delicious combination of all the above de-stressing activities? Draw a hot bath. Turn off the phones. Pour a cocktail. Light a fragrant candle and reach for a great book you can't put down. Soak luxuriously while turning the pages. A minivacation!

- Finally, I love to cook. Just being in the kitchen preparing a casual meal or a complicated dessert can be equally relaxing and rewarding.

3 . . . 2 . . . 1 . . . Countdown to a Fabulous Dinner Party

It's All About Timing

When planning a dinner party, do you feel (a) confident, cool, and prepared; or (b) as if you need to host it in a hotel or restaurant? If your answer is *a,* congratulations; you're in good shape. If your answer is *b,* I'm here to help. If you were too nervous and overworked to respond, do yourself a favor and read the rest of this in a hot bubble bath.

- It costs nothing, yet it's the single most crucial element of any celebration: timing! On a piece of paper, jot down a schedule of when guests will arrive, what cocktails you will serve (keep in mind that forty-five minutes to an hour is the ideal time for cocktails before dinner), what music you'll have playing in the background during each part of the evening, when guests will be seated for dinner, when to offer dessert and what needs to happen in between. A schedule of preparty preparation and a during-the-event, minute-by-minute time line will help keep the party going!

- Get organized! Tackle the preparation bit by bit. Make lists of everything you need to buy and do. Refer to these lists often, and cross off items and errands as you go.

- Select a menu. Again, keep it simple but tasteful, including wines and dessert. Determine what ingredients you'll need to buy and where. Figure out how much time it will take to pre-pare each dish, and do as much as possible twenty-four hours before-hand. If it can't be done a day in advance, make sure you have all your washing, peeling, slicing, and dicing done several hours ahead of your guests' arrival. Create an interesting, varied guest list. Try to mix and match groups of friends and intro-duce new people.

- Use Post-it notes to remind yourself where each dish will go on your table. Label plates and serving dishes for each course to avoid last-minute confusion (see the Entertaining Gal-lery, pages 188–189).

- Plan your table setting. Decide on which china and linens you're going to use. Make notes on the colors and types of flowers and other decorative items to buy. Set the table as far in advance as possible. Clean and pol-

There Is a Rock Opera in My Head: Remedies for Hangover Hell

If you have overindulged, I recommend arming yourself with a "cocktail" that will prevent a splitting headache and queasy stomach. Ideally, you should remedy the situation the same night, before going to bed: Take a multivitamin and two aspirin, and drink a tall glass of water to stay hydrated. But if you forget (or fall asleep on the couch), and wake up feeling twenty years older and completely unable to function, then it's Bieler's Broth to the rescue! Originally created in Switzerland, Bieler's Broth is made up of three-fourths of a cup apiece of zucchini, chopped celery, green beans, and parsley. Steam them over hot distilled water, five to eight minutes apiece, until they're soft but still crisp. Using a blender, puree the steamed vegetables with a portion of the steaming water until the contents are almost liquefied. Drink up! The broth coats your stom-ach with alkaline almost immediately, so you'll feel 110 percent better.

For your puffy, bloodshot eyes, lie down flat on a bed or couch with your feet elevated. Place a comfort-able pillow under your head. Close your eyes and gently lay a couple of warm teabags (not too hot, not too cold) over them. After ten minutes, the tea will seep into your skin, diminishing the circles under your eyes and help-ing to remove the red. Let's not even attempt to figure out how this other puffy-eye cure was discovered, but believe it or not, patting a little hemorrhoid cream under your eyes *does* help.

A Hands-On Experience:
The Joys of Massage

Massage was once considered an indulgence reserved exclusively for the rich. Today it's no longer a luxury but a necessity. Whether you're having a deep-tissue massage from a loved one or a professional, hot stone, or Swedish massage, massage is a great way to charge your battery. Here are a few ways to get the most from your massage:

- If the masseuse is coming into your home, be ready with some soothing music. (Create your own CD of relaxing massage-friendly music.) If the massage is taking place outside your home, bring along your own soundtrack or iPod.

- If at home, light a candle—or two, or three—and if you like, a stick of incense.

- Make sure that the room is the right temperature.

- If you have an extremely talkative massage therapist and are not in the mood for chitchat, explain your need for silence.

- Keep slippers near the massage table so you don't leave oil marks on the floors or the carpet, or worse, slip on a tiled bathroom floor.

- If you're pleased with your massage, tip the massage therapist 15 percent of the fee.

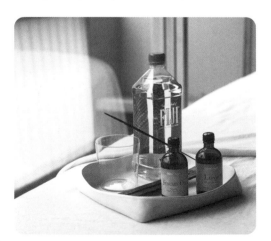

ish your serving pieces a day or two before the party.

- Music is the ultimate mood enhancer. If you have a CD changer, program a variety of CDs for random play so you won't have to worry about constantly changing the music. If you own an iPod and speakers, create your own playlist for the evening. You'll want something lively for the cocktail hour to encourage conversation, and something more subdued and instrumental during dinner. Try some light opera or Billie Holiday for dessert and coffee. The key is to keep the music playing from the moment your guests arrive until the door closes behind them.

- Sear steaks or fish or chicken before the guests arrive. The food can continue cooking in the oven while you're finishing your first course with your guests. The messy dishes have already been cleared (either by you or a discreet catering staff), and you are finishing the cooking in the oven on a foil disposable container!

- Design a flow for cocktail parties. I love orchestrating small vignettes, or stations—self-contained areas where I can place food along with appropriate drinks. This creates an easy flow of traffic, allows for multiple conversation zones, and keeps my guests from having to wait in line around a single buffet table.

- If you plan to order part (or all!) of the food you'll be serving, confirm the delivery or pickup time with the restaurant, chef, or caterer.

- At a sit-down dinner for parties of more than eight guests, place cards are helpful. They prevent confusion or awkwardness, and allow you to balance the energy and dynamics of the table. Separating spouses also makes for freer and more lively conversation. Remember, for a guest to rearrange his or her host's place cards is an offense punishable by death!

- If at all possible, try to leave yourself with next to nothing to do the day of the party aside from putting the finishing touches on your food. Ideally, you won't have to leave the house that day! In my mind, the best moment is that half hour before guests arrive, when you can freshen up and make the transition that transforms you from chief cook and glass washer to host. Failing that, a splash of water, fresh makeup, a clean blouse or shirt, or a change of shoes can do the trick if time is of the essence. Now you're ready to move into the all-important preparation phase.

Before the Doorbell Rings

Make sure you're ready for your guests *before* the doorbell rings. Depending on the season and the time of day, you may have set out a pitcher of lemonade or a pitcher of your favorite Chili Passion Martinis or a bottle of vintage Champagne. The table should be set, the lights dimmed, and your iPod hooked up and playing. Appetizers should be ready, whether it's an assortment of cheeses, a bowl of exotic olives or nuts, or perhaps something completely unexpected and decadent, like a log of foie gras and a loaf of brioche.

Now greet your guests at the door with a huge smile! Take their coats and offer them a drink ASAP! The more prepared you are, the more the room will come alive, and the more welcome your guests will feel.

A Refreshing Restroom: Bathroom Niceties

- When I'm planning on having friends over (which is any-time I can), I make sure to prepare the bathroom for my guests. I covered all this in the section on preparing my bathroom for overnight guests (page 87). But do remem-ber to check the condition of the bathroom several times during the evening. It's essential that you keep it clean all night long, and that there be extra hand towels, extra tissues, extra soap, extra everything!

- If I'm employing a staff, I'll ask one of my workers to per-form this same task of maintenance. I keep a basket filled with air freshener, cleaner, and paper towels standing by and ready to make it easy for the room to be cleaned at a moment's notice. You can store the supplies under the sink or keep them in a cabinet close by. If you only have one bathroom for a very large group of guests, make sure you have an attendant to keep it clean at all times, or dou-ble up on your own tidying efforts as the night goes on.

Master of Your Domain: Informal Meal Basics

As a host, part of my repertoire includes a half dozen signature dishes: dishes that are tasty, fun, and fairly easy to prepare. Everybody needs to develop a repertoire. It could be a killer New York steak and arugula salad. Or a crispy roasted chicken. Or a fresh Caesar salad with garlicky croutons. Whatever your favorites, stick with what you know, and do not confuse dinner guests with guinea pigs. The tried-and-true recipes are always best. Feel free to experiment on your own. If your heart is set on something new, try the recipe in advance so you're comfortable instead of stressed when it's time for the dish's public debut.

Size Matters: Seating Your Guests

- As a rule, I like to keep the table settings tight so everyone rubs elbows and the meal feels intimate. In my dining room

I maintain two separate square tables. Depending on how many guests I've invited over that night, I can comfortably seat anywhere from four to twelve people. If I rent round tables, I know I can seat six to eight people at a fifty-four-inch, eight to ten at a sixty-inch, and ten to twelve at a sixty-six-inch. Anything larger and it becomes too hard to make conversation with anyone other than the people directly to your left and your right. Talk always flows better when the energy is tight and contained.

- If, like most people, you have a big dining room with a single large table, consider renting (or even purchasing) two narrow — no more than forty-eight inches across — tables, rather than one, that can be joined with ease. And if you're having a small dinner party, seat everyone close together at one table or at one end and set the wines and waters at the other. This looks lush and plentiful and allows everyone to chat.

Setting Pretty: Formally and Informally

Whether I'm entertaining a half dozen people or ten people or more, I've gotten my seating arrangements down pat. Here are a few basics.

For six, ten, or fourteen people:

- If I'm hosting a party in someone's honor, I will always sit at the head of the table with the guest of honor seated directly to my right. If you are a hostess, and feting a male guest of honor, seat him directly to your right. The hostess should sit at the end of the table, nearest the kitchen, with the host at the opposite end.

For eight, twelve, or sixteen people:

- In this instance, the hostess should move one place to the left and seat the male guest of honor directly to her right, opposite the host. This way you avoid seating two women and two men together.

- Formal dining may not be part of daily life, but a gracious host always serves his female guests first! And himself last.

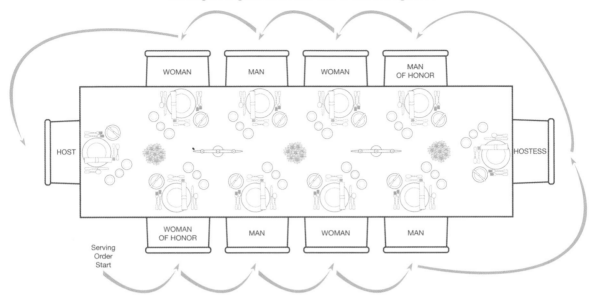

seating arrangement for six, ten, or fourteen guests

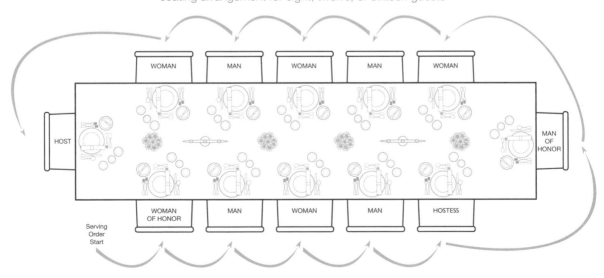

seating arrangement for eight, twelve, or sixteen guests

Table Basics, Formal and Informal

It's the twenty-first century. Do you know where your finger bowl is? Of course not! Unless you happen to live in Windsor Castle, you're probably not going ultraformal at home, though there are times when you probably feel like pulling out all the stops. Here's how I set the table for both casual and more straitlaced occasions (remember, these traditions are as old as entertaining itself and were originally created for a world of right-handed people):

The Silver Lining: Plates and Flatware

- If I'm entertaining formally, I will set down decorative chargers, which serve as placeholders and anchor each place setting. For informal occasions, I bypass the chargers and simply set out my dinner plates.

- I'll often place a folded napkin atop the charger or dinner plate (see a few more napkin options on pages 166–167).

- I position flatware in the logical order of its use, to the left or right of the plate, beginning from the outside in; in other words, moving toward the plate. Thus, guests will use the outermost fork for the salad, the middle fork for the fish course, and the innermost fork for the dinner itself. Knives and spoons sit on the right of the plate, again using the same intuitive order. If you're serving a fabulous soup for starters, the soup spoon goes in the outermost position. Assuming you're serving a fish course, place the fish knife in the middle, and the knife closest to the plate is reserved for dinner (make sure you keep the sharp edges of your knives facing *toward* the plate, with the bottoms of your flatware neatly aligned).

- If I'm serving bread with the meal, I place a small bread plate to the left and

"At a seated dinner party, men should remain standing behind their chair until the women are seated. Men, make sure you've introduced yourselves to everyone before taking your seat."

seating arrangement for ten guests at a 60" round table

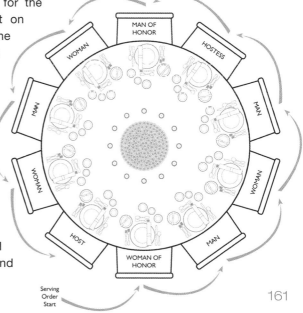

slightly above the dinner plate, and lay the butter knife diagonally across the bottom.

- If I'm serving dessert, I place the dessert fork and the dessert spoon right above the plate.

- When everybody is finished, I clear all of the dinner settings away and bring out the after-dinner items: dessert plates and, if I'm serving coffee, a tray of cups and saucers along with teaspoons, which rest either on the saucers or on the table (your choice).

- Very simply, informal meals require less of everything. You don't need to go the whole nine yards. Position a salad fork and a dinner fork to the left of the plate, a single knife to the right, and you have the basics for a casual meal.

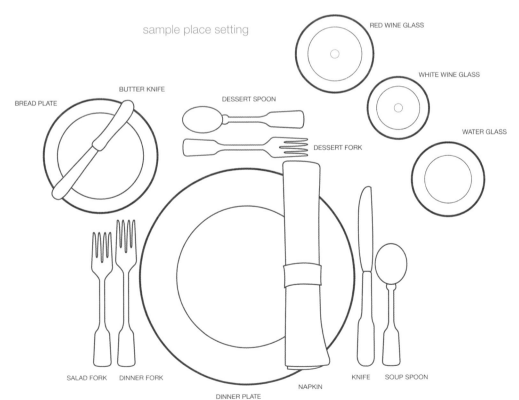

sample place setting

RED WINE GLASS

WHITE WINE GLASS

WATER GLASS

BUTTER KNIFE

BREAD PLATE

DESSERT SPOON

DESSERT FORK

SALAD FORK   DINNER FORK

NAPKIN

KNIFE   SOUP SPOON

DINNER PLATE

Setting a Buffet Table

Buffets work for both small and large gatherings, particularly the latter. They're casual, easy, and give you the opportunity to showcase your creativity and sense of theater.

- A buffet should look abundant! If the table is large, group everything together rather than spreading out the food. At the other end of the table, place florals or set up a bar or coffee and dessert. Instant celebration!

- A well-balanced buffet should offer a vegetable, a protein, a salad, a grain-based dish, and a bread. For summertime, set out a platter of poached salmon, a cucumber sauce, a plate of poached asparagus, a crisp salad, potatoes or rice, and a crunchy baguette—and call it a day!

- For a more lavish buffet, offer multiples of each category. If you're serving both meats and fishes, keep them on separate buffets so their sauces don't mix. I have never been a lover of "surf and turf" (you saw my cardinal rule on page 136); however, if space is limited and you have to offer both on one table, set the fish with the salad and rice at one side of the buffet, a centerpiece in the middle, and the meat, salad, and potatoes on the other side. Place your plates, napkins, and silverware at each end.

- Put the clean plates at the beginning of your buffet, followed by the cold items. Next come the hot entrées. Last should be the silverware and napkins (so your guests won't be juggling napkins, forks, knives, and spoons while trying to fill their plates). If you have enough room, set a bar at the other end of the table, with bottles of wine and glasses waiting for your guests to help themselves.

- At outdoor buffets, keep the food covered until you're ready to dine, and set out enough citronella candles to keep any bugs at bay.

No White Bread, Pasta, Potatoes, or Rice—I Swear It Works!

By now everyone knows that diets have a high failure rate and usually don't work. Eating healthily is a lifelong decision and requires a lifestyle change. I don't care how many carbs you're depriving yourself of, or if you're consuming only mandarin orange segments and kelp during the day, diets are exclusively for the short-term. Period!

Instead of diets, I recommend embracing a lifestyle that will get you to your target weight, and keep you there *without* deprivation.

As a charter member of the food business, I'm always racing around attending food and wine tastings, and developing and sampling the recipes from my entertaining books, as well as for the weddings and events I plan. If I ate absolutely everything I wanted, I would be the size of a house. When I was twenty-nine years old, my waist measured 29 inches. When I was thirty, my waist kept pace at 30 inches. When my waist and I both reached 32, I realized that if I kept going at this rate, I'd someday have to be buried in a grand-piano box. It was time for me to develop a sensible daily eating program that was healthy, delicious, maintainable, and that would never, ever make me feel deprived.

Today my waist measures a compact 30 inches, and I weigh 153 pounds, which I'm proud to say is approximately 2 pounds less than what I weighed when I arrived in this country in 1985. I abstain from absolutely nothing. I never think to myself, *I'm on a diet.* Instead, if asked, I tell people that I am engaged in a healthy, nutritious lifestyle that involves daily mindfulness and daily decision-making.

The most important element of my daily eating habits is *negotiation with myself.* Meaning that every single day of my life, I make low-carb, high-protein decisions and strive for balance. If I've overindulged in the morning, then I won't partake of something rich that evening. If I've been good all day, then that night I'll help myself to several spoonfuls of a decadent chocolate mousse, or a small slice of key lime cheesecake. The trick is to be mindful, and to make intelligent, conscious choices about what I eat.

The following lifestyle approach to eating works for me and so many of my friends and colleagues, I'm positive it'll make a difference in your life, too. As a general rule: no white bread, potatoes, or rice (though I do allow myself a small portion of pasta on very special occasions). Here's my plan:

- Eat a minimum of three to four meals a day. If you jump-start your morning by eating a healthy breakfast within ninety minutes of waking up, it will ensure a faster metabolic rate all day. Breakfast needn't be boring, either, if you vary what you eat. On Monday, try a blueberry smoothie. On Tuesday, prepare a small cheese omelet, using more egg whites than yolks. On Wednesday, prepare a B.L.T. using nonfat Canadian bacon, a slice of fresh lettuce, a couple slices of tomato, a poached egg or two, some low-fat mayo, a pinch of rock salt, and two slices of Ezekiel, rye, or wheat bread (any kind that isn't made from white flour). Instead of feeling deprived, you'll feel as though you've gone to heaven.

- My general advice to dieters everywhere: Avoid white! White pastries, white bread, white sugar, white rice. White foods will pack on the pounds, deplete your energy, and make you feel on the verge of a twenty-year nap. Whenever possible, prepare a sandwich on multigrain, seed, or Ezekiel bread rather than on white. If you're a longtime rice lover, eat brown or wild rice. Want something really delicious? I suggest taking a bursting ripe tomato, stuffing it with savory cooked brown rice, topping it with some Parmesan cheese, then placing it under the broiler.

- I haven't completely eliminated pasta from my diet. I *adore* pasta—I believe it's one of life's greatest pleasures. But I limit my intake of pasta that's made from white flour to perhaps once a month, when I will treat myself to a small portion at a great Italian restaurant, or else I'll share a bowl of pasta with a dinner guest. If I'm going to indulge myself, I make sure that I eat a truly memorable bowl of pasta and not just pasta for pasta's sake. While I limit my white-flour pasta intake to special occasions, I often eat buckwheat pasta or noodles, which are a thousand times better for you!

- Never deprive yourself. Deprivation leads to a domino effect: The second you feel deprived, the munchies will overtake you, followed by a lightning storm of inner turmoil . . . then, when you feel as though you've just lost the battle, you think, Why not eat that entire chocolate cake and two gallons of ice cream while I'm at it? A lot of people sabotage their eating programs right then and there. If you want a piece of bread, choose a healthy multi-grain brown bread and just don't have more than two slices!

- Weigh yourself every day. I do. That way, if I've put on a couple of pounds over the weekend when I tend to be a little more lenient on myself, then I know that the no-nos aren't an option for me over the next few days. If I'm down a couple of pounds, then I feel free to order a hamburger with a side of toasted wheat or rye bread and a small order of French fries. It's all about negotiating the proper balance and dining consciously, day by day. And if you're working out, remember that muscle weighs more than fat, so don't punish yourself if you look great in the mirror but your weight seems to have hit an all-time high. Judge your appearance by how well your clothes fit rather than by an increase on the scale.

- If you're planning on drinking wine in the evening—and I love nothing more than an after-work cocktail and a couple glasses of great wine over dinner—then abstain from soda during the day. A can of Coke contains close to 12 tablespoons of sugar. Just one less soda a day and the odds of losing weight will increase as quickly as your confidence level. I drink only water and unsweetened teas when the sun is up . . . and reserve my liquid calories for when the sun goes down.

- Dine consciously. Instead of French fries, I often order a small salad. Alternately, when the French fries arrive, I avoid temptation by taking half and asking the waiter or waitress to take away the rest (because I know that once I start eating them, it's hard to stop). The same goes for the basket of delicious breads. Limit yourself to one piece.

- Feel free to snack during the day, but don't snack on carbohydrate-rich munchies that do nothing but add inches to your waistline. During the day, if I get hungry, I snack on toasted nuts, fresh fruit, or some low-carb soy chips. There are also excellent sugar-free candies and chocolates out there for sweets aficionados. Cheese and lean proteins also make excellent snacks. Just use conscious portion control.

(continued)

- Try to eat lean protein at every meal, with vegetables and grains on the side—and by grains, I mean anything from brown rice to tabouli to lentils to bulgur wheat. At a restaurant, if you're eyeing the grilled sole, ask the waiter if it comes with a side order of rice or potatoes, then see if you can substitute a side of vegetables or salad instead.

- When dessert time comes around, I share a dessert with another person at the table. I don't need to polish off the whole thing! Or, rather than overly rich sweets, I order a bowl of fresh berries or assorted fruits, fruit desserts, a sorbet, or even a half-slice of flourless chocolate cake (tell the waiter you'll pay for the whole, but to bring only half).

- Saturday is my free day. If I can maintain my weight from Monday through Friday, I *deserve* to have a little fun on Saturday. I might have a risotto at lunch, or French-fried onion rings with dinner. I might partake of the most sinful triple-layer-cake ever devised. But by Sunday, I'm back on track, getting into the swing of negotiation.

"For me when I entertain at home on a regular basis for up to 6 guests, it's like doing yoga—pure meditation, completely effortless. Anything more than 6 guests requires a lot more effort. 10-plus becomes a production!"

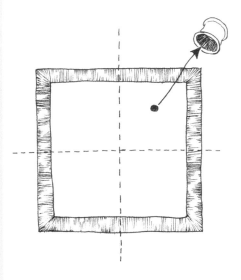

Simple Napkin Choices

As the host, one of your jobs is to set the most beautiful table possible. Among your most basic and versatile tools? The napkin. Create a chic, elegant napkin setting for any occasion with the following examples:

Centerpieces: Chic and Easy

A centerpiece is the focal point of your table. It should give your guests something mesmerizingly beautiful to look at (aside from one another).

There's no need for your centerpiece to be expensive, custom-made from fresh flowers and Tibetan berries, or ornate or overblown.

Centerpiece Dos and Don'ts

1. Your centerpiece shouldn't be more than twelve inches high. Guests should be able to easily make eye contact with one another. The exception to the height rule is when you have a very tall centerpiece with a thin middle, such as a topiary.

2. Instead of filling a large vase with dozens of fresh-cut blooms, consider featuring a single flowering plant or a hardy tropical leaf in an architectural or sculptural organic-shaped vase with a small opening at the top. Think about layering multiple elements to fill the center of the table instead of one large arrangement.

1st napkin fold
The most classic and simple of all napkin folds is a folded napkin with a ring around the middle.

2nd napkin fold
For something more elegant, fold the napkin with a point at the bottom.

3rd napkin fold
My favorite is a simple, flat napkin folded in a rectangle, perhaps with a bowl on top of it.

4th napkin fold
If I'm working with a printed menu, I'll sometimes fold it so I can tuck the napkin into it.

5th napkin fold
For casual entertaining, I pull the napkin through the ring (see illustrations, opposite). To make your napkin appear larger, pull it through the top quadrant instead of the middle, which will result in a longer-looking napkin.

fearless entertaining

3. If you pack a small vase abundantly with lots of flowers, you will make a very lavish impression.

4. Try using a variety of short and tall vases with a different variety of flower in each one. Your goal is to create a beautiful, interesting image—a story, almost—through the sum of all its parts.

5. If you're using fresh flowers, change the water daily so they stay alive as long as possible. If your flowers look droopy, slice a small piece off the stems at an angle so they can hydrate more efficiently.

6. I prefer not to use scented candles on the dining table or buffet, because their fragrance can interfere with the aromas of the food. I say this on behalf of anyone who's ever been overwhelmed by the scent of gardenia while attempting to enjoy a Dover sole.

(For more ideas and inspirations about centerpieces, see the Entertaining Gallery, pages 190–194.)

Regal Events: Formal Entertaining

The truly formal occasion at home is rare these days, since so few homes can accommodate the traditional trappings (even the British royal family and the White House have relaxed the rules). But there are still times that call for a bit of grandeur and lots of style!

The Pleasure of Your Company: Formal Invitations

Formal invitations are either professionally engraved or handwritten on relatively conservative paper. Use them for dinner or luncheon parties, formal dances, cocktail receptions, weddings, or events in honor of special guests.

Send out formal invitations four to six weeks before the event. Guests should reply no later than two weeks in advance.

Acknowledging a Formal Invitation

Reply promptly with a handwritten note. If you are sending regrets to someone who is not a close friend, do so as briefly as possible ("We regret we will be out of town" or "We are unable to attend due to a prior engagement"), but if you are close to the host or hostess, you should also elaborate in the note and call, explaining your absence in more personal terms. If you RSVP that you are coming, then you must go. Period! A yes means that the host is going to decide where you will be best seated, make a place for you at the table, prepare a meal for you, and rely upon your presence. Show up and be on time!

Although people rarely accept invitations to sit-down dinners and then don't show up, I hear many complaints that "no-shows" are fairly typical at cocktail receptions. Hosts have often previously arranged a costly per person head count, often with a caterer. Of those who don't show up, 5 percent call the next day, another 5 percent send a note or an e-mail to apologize or explain, and the other 90 percent of absentees don't bother, leaving the host or hostess upset. It's much better to RSVP with regrets than accept and not go. Never let down anyone who's been throughtful and gracious enough to include you.

Be a Gifted Giver

Whether you're attending an informal cocktail party or an informal dinner, it's customary to bring a gift to your host and/or hostess. Give your host something he or she would enjoy using, or something he or she would not think of buying for himself or herself. Don't bring a gift that has to be tended to immediately like a large bouquet of stunning flowers. As much as it's a lovely thought, your host would then need to unwrap them, snap the stems, hunt down an appropriate vase, and then arrange them, all the while keeping an eye on roasting chickens and a pitcher of cocktails that needs refilling. If you want to send flowers, send them earlier in the day or the following day, accompanied by a note (ideally and most impressive, one that's been handwritten).

On a similar note, don't show up bearing baked goods, either, unless you're visiting a close friend. Chances are your hosts already have that night's menu planned, and you'll make them feel obligated to include your chocolate mousse unless you called ahead.

Fail-proof gifts include a great bottle of wine or Champagne (an old standby, as I mentioned before), a fragrant candle, a favorite book, or a groovy CD. Your host can choose to open, pop in, and play your gift if it fits the evening, or write your name on the wine bottle's label, stow it away for another time, and drink a toast to you at a later date.

You can also dazzle your host with a favorite cookbook, a candy dish filled with candies, a box of chic stationery, a just-released DVD, or a book you love that you know your host will enjoy, too.

Some Dos and Don'ts of Host and Hostess Gifts

1. Ten points for sending in advance a bouquet of flowers or a gorgeous box of gift-wrapped chocolate truffles to your hosts, telling them how much you are looking forward to your visit. Or send them the day after with a fun anecdote you experienced at the party.

2. Leave some of your personalized stationery with the florist, wine merchant, or chocolatier you use regularly. Whenever you want to send a gift, simply dictate a message to be attached to the gift on your letterhead. This scores many points with minimal effort!

3. Always be on the lookout for creative gifts to buy and store for future hostess gifts. A few of my favorites include lovely bottles of imported olive oils, flavored vinegars, luscious honeys, and wonderful jams. Of course, a good bottle of wine or Champagne is appropriate for almost any occasion.

4. Avoid regifting, particularly if you navigate a small social circle. What a bittersweet surprise for your host to receive the very same box of rosewater Turkish delight.

Everyday Niceties Go a Long Way

At the Party

The gracious host . . . always helps a woman on and off with her coat, holds the door for her, stands until she takes her seat at the table, lights her cigarette if she smokes, and offers to fetch her a drink if she's empty-handed (the same holds true for male guests!).

The considerate guest . . . makes eye contact with the other guests and states his name clearly when introducing himself. He also repeats the name of the person he is meeting, to make sure he's heard it correctly. He can also use the person's name to segue into more specific conversation; for example, "I have a wonderful friend who's also named Sheila. I was just speaking with her, and we were laughing about the time we . . . "

The gracious host . . . omits job titles when introducing people in nonbusiness situations, since doing so would imply he defines them exclusively by what they do for a living. (There are exceptions, however. If a host is introducing a prominent person, such as a judge or a member of the clergy, it's a mark of respect to use their job title: for example, "Justice Samuels," or "Reverend Thomas Means.")

The considerate guest . . . focuses on the person he's talking to, and *focusing* means more than nodding your head and mumbling yes every few seconds. It means listening and engaging.

The gracious host . . . makes it easy on herself and those with her by always introducing others as soon as possible to include them in her conversations.

The considerate guest . . . knows how to exit a conversation if it's swiping more of his time than his attention span allows, saying: "I'm sorry to cut you off, but I see a friend whom I've been trying to get ahold of for some weeks. Would you mind if I excuse myself?"

The gracious host . . . never leaves a conversation with an uncomfortable vibe floating in the air.

The considerate guest . . . knows that there's no such thing as being fashionably late, only unfashionably tardy! An eight o'clock invitation to an intimate dinner party means

eight o'clock, which allows time for cocktails and a sit-down dinner at eight-forty-five. It doesn't mean that he can breeze through the door at eight-forty-five! If the guest knows he'll be detained, he should call his host immediately, apologize, let him know his projected arrival time, and avoid long-winded explanations. P.S.: Showing up too early is as inconvenient to the host as arriving late! And a guest should never, *ever* bring uninvited guests along without clearing it with his hosts beforehand! Also, if he receives an invitation that does not specifically say "and guest," or, alternatively, if he and his wife or partner have children and the invitation does not specifically mention their names on the envelope, they should not bring along the children, or attempt to solicit another invitation.

There *are* exceptions to this rule, however. Sometimes hosts simply aren't aware of your living situation, that is, that you're married, or have been sharing your life with a longtime partner. Gently remind them of this—"May I invite my partner of eighteen years?"—and nine times out of ten, the two of you will end up attending the occasion arm in arm.

To the Table!

The gracious host . . . asks his guests beforehand if they have any dietary restrictions. If a couple keeps kosher, or if the host is aware that their culture or diet has dietary guidelines, the host asks exactly what they can and cannot eat. Fad dieters should eat their head of cabbage and eleven grapefruits beforehand and not expect anything special!

The considerate guest . . . refrains from bringing glassware from the cocktail party to the dinner table. When she excuses herself from the table during a meal, she leaves her napkin on her chair. Only when the meal is done, and she's getting ready to leave, should she put a used napkin on the table. If she's having red sauce while wearing white, she should feel free to hold the napkin across her chest to protect herself against any unexpected splatters, but should avoid tucking it inside her collar or neckline. (The only exception to this rule is if she's eating crabs or lobster, and sitting casually with friends). In general, guests should use their napkins exclusively for wiping their lips and hands, and throughout a meal to dab at the corners of their mouths whenever necessary. Women should never use their napkins to blot their lipstick (use a separate tissue)—I have seen this too many times and always cringe when I see never-to-be-removed Ferrari-red lips on a white linen napkin.

The gracious host . . . deals with tardy guests by keeping on schedule with the dinner after removing the late guest's place setting. If the guest shows up half an hour later, murmuring a traffic excuse, the host should greet his late arrival warmly and make the proper allowances, even if it means squeezing in an extra chair . . . and he should feel free to then think twice about inviting that person again.

The considerate guest . . . refrains from taking a seat until the hostess and most of the other women have been seated first.

The gracious host . . . separates spouses around the table (they have the rest of their lives to chat with each other!) and seats men next to women. This helps balance the energy in the room and makes for more sparkling conversation. However, there are a few exceptions. If the host is giving a party for someone, he seats his guest of honor directly to his right. If a couple is hosting the event, one spouse sits to the left of the guest of honor, and the other to the right.

The considerate guest . . . has reverence for the bond that's created when people are seated at a dinner table and makes every effort to take any bathroom visits or cigarette breaks before being seated.

The gracious host . . . serves the women at the table first. Usually, the hostess is the last woman served before the men are served. The host serves from the left and clears from the right. A good host will ask guests to begin dining when three or more plates are on the table. A lot of time, thought, and energy went into the food preparation, and the meal should be enjoyed while it is still hot. If there are six or eight guests, the host waits for the entire table to finish before he begins clearing, or else guests will feel rushed.

The considerate guest . . . knows that good table manners are meant to be invisible—and are a profound reflection of who you are! Therefore, he avoids slouching, leaning, lying,

Twenty-First-Century
Finger Bowls . . .

Try placing lavender oil and a slice of lemon in warm water in a shallow glass. Or provide wet, lemon-doused napkins or hand towels warmed in the microwave in plastic wrap or chilled from the refrigerator or freezer. Roll the napkins tightly and serve them on a tray, or on a bamboo mat beside each plate, Japanese style.

or resting his elbows and arms on the table, and instead maintains an elegant posture with his shoulders back. He eats and drinks silently, never slurps, takes small bites, chews his food well, and, naturally, never attempts to speak if he has food in his mouth. If he's just taken a bite and someone asks him a question, a simple finger held in the air speaks volumes!

The gracious host . . . engages her guests, monitors the flow of the conversation, and does her best not to let one person dominate. If the conversation is lacking, she picks a current subject—a hot movie, an article she's just read, a vacation destination—to get people animated. She steers as clear as possible away from politics and religion!

The considerate guest . . . turns his head away when coughing or sneezing and places his napkin over his mouth. He never burps or blows his nose at the table. If the guest needs to wash his hands, and his host hasn't offered a warm napkin, hand towel, or equivalent, he should use his own napkin, or excuse himself and refresh himself in the bathroom.

The gracious host . . . serves one to two glasses of wine per course and offers a preferred nonalcoholic beverage to those who do not drink.

The considerate guest . . . always accepts the offer of a drink. If he doesn't drink alcohol, he should say, "Thank you, I'd love to have a glass of something nonalcoholic, possibly sparkling water." But he shouldn't refuse the offering; by doing so, he removes himself from the ritual that everyone else is sharing, and he should be able to raise his glass during a toast.

The gracious host . . . stops serving drinks to an obviously intoxicated guest. If the guest's behavior is insulting to others, the hostess might ask the guest to come into another room with her and ask him to tone it down. If someone is extremely rude and obnoxious, the hostess is free to ask him to leave, though a hostess should never let someone who's had too much to drink drive home. Call for a cab or car service, or accept another guest's offer to drive the person home. A hostess should expect an apology the following morning, or feel free to remove the offender from her Rolodex.

"My father was the life of the party. He always knew how to make people feel comfortable, what to say, and when to say it."

An Attitude of Gratitude for Hospitality and Gifts

You had a fantastic time, thanks to the effort and trouble your host went through, and it's better to acknowledge hospitality sooner rather than later. A handwritten thank-you note on personalized stationery wins you maximum points; it takes only a few minutes, and it makes your host or hostess feel appreciated. A phone call first thing the next morning is thoughtful and appropriate. But if for some reason you're unable to say thank you in either of those ways, you can also send a fax, an e-mail, an e-card, or leave a voice-mail message. The most important factor is the acknowledgment, and the thank-you itself. It's never too late. You might find two weeks went by and you just did not have the time. Go ahead and send a note now—it's *always* the right thing to do.

Thank-you notes can be brief, but they should be both prompt and genuine. Find something real and heartfelt to say, then communicate it with as much sincerity and gusto as possible. If you like, feel free to write a thank-you note in addition to an e-mailed or telephoned thanks. When we check the mail, the first thing we always do is look for the handwritten note.

The following situations demand a thank-you note:

- **Dinner Parties:** If someone is throwing a party in your honor, or even if you are just a guest, send a handwritten note. For extra points, send flowers or a gift either before or afterward (see pages 169–70 for more advice on host and hostess gifts).

- **Receipt of a Gift:** Even if you have already said thank you in person, send a handwritten note or call the very next morning.

- **Get Well Notes:** For someone who's ill, receiving a card or note can be more important than you realize.

- **Condolences:** Many people are uncomfortable expressing their condolences. They have no idea what to say, so they opt for silence instead. If you are a close personal friend of the bereaved, pick up the phone. If you aren't as close, or don't have an established telephone relationship, then write a note, make a donation in someone's memory, or send flowers. The gesture will be tremendously comforting.

- **Congratulations:** Always celebrate life's milestones. A note will convey your best thoughts, happiest wishes, and general pleasure. When someone does well, succeeds, or triumphs, nothing feels better to the recipient than an acknowledgment! Certain occasions always call for a congratulatory gesture: graduating from high school or college, landing a new job, getting a promotion or closing a deal, the birth of a child, a move, a prize won. A handwritten note is welcome and ideal, but a phone call, e-mail, fax, flowers, or a bottle of good Champagne work just as well. The point is to mark and commemorate the moment.

It's best to discuss the situation the following day when the guest is in a clear state of mind, not intoxicated. You will never win an argument with a person who is roaring drunk, and the situation will go from unfortunate to ugly.

The considerate guest . . . never applies makeup at the table unless it's lipstick, which can be applied discreetly. If women want to touch up all their makeup, they should do so in the ladies' room beforehand or afterward.

The gracious host . . . signals that the dinner party is over by getting up from the table, which gives guests unofficial license to leave. If guests are still lingering, he can be more direct: "I hope you'll excuse me, I have an early day tomorrow." Coffee and a tray of cookies also signal, subtly, when a dinner party has come to an end. The moment the host gets up from the table, one or two people will find an excuse to leave, and a few more will find their way to the living room. Considerate guests should take their cue from other guests. If the host's closet friends are lingering over after-dinner gossip with the host and clearing the last of the plates, he can afford to say, "I need to get some sleep, but thanks so much, and let's talk in the morning."

"When deciding on the time for your party, consider the basics . . . the bigger the city, the later the acceptable dinner time . . . there are more things to squeeze into each night, and a late dinner is often welcomed!"

entertaining
gallery

1–2 When it comes to dressing a table, let your imagination (and the seasons) be your guide. Here, fall was interpreted in a minimalist way.

3 There's nothing quite so dramatic as a splash of red flowers, especially on a piano.

4 A table topped with a mirror, simple white china paired with ornate silver, and an orchid greet guests at this glamorous dinner.

1 Placing a single blossom in a small floral vase, then setting multiples down the center of the table, makes for an inexpensive yet lavish centerpiece.

2 One of my favorite times to entertain is during the summer months, when we get to entertain outdoors.

3 Shaken, not stirred! There's nothing like a good stiff cocktail to take your mood from drab to fab. Note the couture ice cube in my martini glass.

1 For an afternoon get-together, I set a beautiful table on the patio and prepare a delicious lunch for a few close friends.

2 A store-bought salad is enhanced with a sliced, diced, home-cooked chicken breast.

3 Just a splash! Here's where Colin's Vinaigrette comes in handy (see recipe on page 37).

4 No fuss, no stress. This stylish glassware is elegant and casual at the same time.

5 These beautiful napkin rings were a gift from my mother, Gloria (she always knows a good accessory when oho oooo ono).

6 Simple pleasures: Even a casual lunch outdoors is more inviting when the table is set with linen napkins and place mats.

7 Cheers! A toast to good friends, great conversation, and a delicious meal. *Bon appétit.*

1 My living room at Christmas: By working with a single color and adding equal doses of glamour and elegance, I'm able to give it a sleek contemporary look.

2 Even a silver-dusted candle can be dressed up for the holiday when surrounded by silver ornaments and white roses.

3 Crystals, votives, and tight bunches of silver-flocked branches come together to create a beautiful arrangement on top of my piano.

4 Candle-scape of tapers and votives is accented with fragrant white roses, Amaryllis, carnations, and white peonies.

5 My own Winter Wonderland: a silver and white tree—to me, the most glamorous Christmas tree imaginable.

6 I feel like James Bond. Here I'm surrounded by the talented ladies who work for me. As usual, we're having way too much fun!

7 At Christmas, I turn my home office into a fully loaded bar by covering my desk with beautiful holiday linens and clearing out my bookcase and replacing my books with glasses. The silver ornament topiaries added just the right touch—clearly an all-around OTT (over-the-top) event!

1 For a colorful dinner party, it's all about mixing and less about matching: an expensive array of St. Louis lavender glasses placed next to a $5 silver bowl. And every price range in-between completes the rest of the table.

2 Fresh flowers in vibrant pink set a festive tone.

3 Use notes and diagrams to stay organized.

4 Offer a signature cocktail of the night. I call it my Cocktail du Jour.

5 Set the table for dining and bring the food to the table family-style on large platters for everyone to help themselves.

6 I like to make a note to myself indicating which wine is served with each course.

7 I fashioned this carefully folded Indian sari into a table runner.

8 For an added splash of color and layer of texture, I carefully folded a napkin to line a white dinner plate.

9 These African horn salt and pepper servers are quite chic!

10 The second course, a crispy salad, came straight from the refrigerator where it had already been placed in individual bowls.

11 Medium-rare lamb served with a melange of spring vegetables is easy to prepare and serve.

1

POTATOES

BEANS

TURKEY   GRAVY   CRANBERRY

MICHAEL

SARA

STUART

COLIN

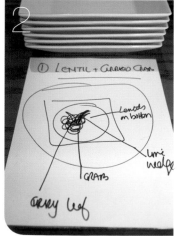

2

① LENTIL + CARROT CURRY

Lentils
on bottom

Lime
wedge

CRABS

CURRY LEAF

3

② Chicken wings +
Crispy Okra

OKRA   SAUCE

Lime
wedge

WINGS

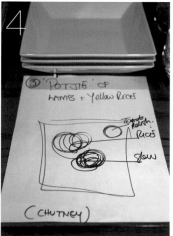

4

③ "POTJIE" OF
LAMB + Yellow Rice

Tomato
Relish

RICE

STEW

(CHUTNEY)

1 Successful entertaining starts with being prepared. The night before a dinner like this, I lay out the different dishes and serving pieces for each course, select my wines, and set the tables. The following day, all I need to do is mix the cocktails, dim the lights, turn up my iPod, and play host.

2–4 Diagrams of how food is served and garnished help me communicate my vision with the kitchen assistants.

5 Moments before going to take a quick shower, I'm double-checking on the placement of my guests' seating.

6 I believe in order in the house. The better prepared you are, the more time you get to spend at the dinner table. The night before, I set out additional serving glasses and label my plates and my serving pieces, so everybody knows what needs to be done, and when.

1 Instead of one large bowl of expensive flowers, this centerpiece consists of some brown silk-covered boxes packed abundantly with carnations, gladiola blossoms, and white hydrangeas—three inexpensive flowers that look lavish arranged this way.

2 Two pieces of glass sculpture and a series of candles make this nonfloral summery centerpiece colorful and mesmerizing.

3 For a colorful look I've filled a decorative bowl with eggplants and limes, and finished it off with a chartreuse Dendrobium blossoms.

4 For another nonfloral look, this mercury installation of pillar candles, reflecting balls, and bowls filled with fruit does the trick.

5 An installation of white flowers, white hydrangea, rose pomanders, and tulips, all arranged on their own . . . along with a single Phaelonopsis blossom.

6 These miniature calla lilies are striking.

7 Ideal for summer, these five-inch cylinders with moss balls have a few simple apples placed graphically between them.

8 These round bamboo planters are filled with growing moss. This centerpiece will last a good six weeks.

9 A large slab of wheatgrass makes for a very fresh and easy centerpiece.

10 These large artichokes were hollowed out and used as candle bases, while the miniatures doubled as place-card holders.

11 The centerpiece is a Lucite trough filled with water and floating Dendrobium blossoms.

12 For a buffet, a bowl of apples was my only centerpiece, brought to life with these colorful napkins and carved napkin rings.

1 This napkin ring was fashioned out of fresh ivy, while wild daisies were fashioned in jam jars for a casual Sunday brunch.

2 A napkin tied with a suede ribbon and a dried leaf with your name written on it is very easy and elegant for a fall soiree.

3 I love layering different mediums of plates. Here we have a very fine and elegant dinner plate topped with a casual terra-cotta plate, finished off with a very fine porcelain and gold bowl.

4 Three different styles of china are placed one atop the other for a very chic, collected look. Small julep cups filled with white roses finish the table.

5 A lovely combination of purple Phaelonopsis orchids together with hydrangea and dahlias are arranged in a jewel-studded Swarovski vase.

6 A simple shamrock mum placed atop a place card on a matching napkin is striking and modern.

7 For a very ethnic feeling, I placed rattan chargers on top of an African kente cloth, and finished off the table with brightly striped napkins and colorful carved African napkin rings.

8 For fall, the layering of reactive glazed china comes alive when I serve my first-course soup in a hollowed-out pumpkin.

9 This centerpiece, a combination of growing moss balls and candles, punctuates a very modern composition.

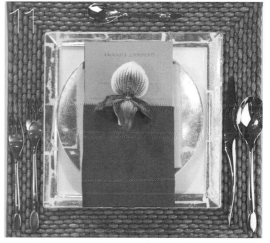

10–12 Three identical place settings, and three different napkin treatments: a very simple rectangular napkin with a round computer-generated postcard sitting on the top third of the napkin; after creating a pocket, we tucked in a customized menu and revved it up with a pristine slipper orchid peeking out the top; a duotone of grosgrain ribbon with a slipknot around it. Nature adds the finishing touch (I used a silver magic marker to inscribe the guest's name on it).

five

work-ethic chic

Ground Rules

Living well means all day, every day, moment by moment. Whether you are traveling to Miami, having a dinner party in your home, or conducting a meeting in your office, the way you navigate your life should be a reflection of you and who you are. Your ability to juggle all of life's tasks and give them your own sense of order and flair shows how much style you have— so keep your image a passionate example shining brightly not just in your home but in your workplace, too.

I have to admit it: I'm a workaholic! I totally love what I do. I've worked from home and also inside a more corporate environment, since my company, Colin Cowie Lifestyle, has offices in both Los Angeles and New York. Though I've never been to management school, over the years I've devised a management system that I consider almost fail-safe.

Passion, teamwork, pride, elegance, efficiency, and humility are the foundations of our success. These characteristics make up the culture of Colin Cowie Lifestyle and are evident in every single one of our ventures.

I believe in (1) leading by example, meaning that I don't expect others to do what I can't do. I show my workers how to carry out the highest standards possible. (2) I set up workplace ground rules and standards of cleanliness, orderliness, promptness, and professionalism; and (3) I motivate my team to bring every last bit of energy, expertise, commitment, and respect to whatever project they're working on. As a result, today my office rivals my home as a welcoming, wonderfully lean machine, with an incomparable staff and the highest possible ratio of output to input (think Swiss watch 24/7)!

A great workplace should not only make your employees

feel inspired to give 120 percent of their energy 100 percent of the time, but it should also make clients and visitors feel welcome, well cared for, and utterly confident that they've landed in the right hands. I believe it all begins at the top. If I commit to going that extra mile—by *always* doing more than what's expected of me—then I can expect my employees to do the same. If I set standards of professionalism and good boundaries between employees and employer, my staff will, too. If I make it absolutely clear from the get-go what I expect from myself and from the people who work for me, my business can't help but surpass *everybody's* expectations. Nowadays our company plans on average four weddings and ten parties a year. The paradox is that the bigger our business becomes, the less work we're able to take on, because the productions we commit to, and the sheer amount of work involved, are typically so enormous and time-consuming that we find ourselves reluctantly turning away countless inquiries!

Confidence is a very important ingredient. It's like salt: Too much will spoil the recipe, and too little produces an uninspiring, weak concoction. But I believe humility is the governing handle on ego. There's a thin line between confidence and arrogance—and every boss and employee has to figure out that line for him- or herself.

With that said, it's important as a manager to understand how to massage the egos of the people who work for me to get the absolute best from them, and the clients for whom I work in order to best understand and satisfy them. I suppose you could call me a top-notch Ego-Masseuse and I am only too happy to oblige! I have *never* believed in screaming and shouting. I find it very belittling. Whenever I witness an outburst of this kind, I always feel embarrassed and sorry for the person doing the screaming. Instead, by working side by side with your staff, and leading them by example with humility, you'll see that there's no limit to how far a motivated staff will go in search of excellence. It's a win-win for everyone. For this reason, I seldom refer to myself as the boss, or prattle on and on about *my* achievements. In the final analysis, Colin Cowie Lifestyle is a *we* business.

Setting Up an Office

I am always impressed with order—and with offices in which everything has its proper place. When bosses and employees know precisely what to expect on a day-to-day basis—where to find expense report forms, how to greet incoming visitors, and how to clean their desk space at the end of the day—an office will run without any bumps in the road. Just as no one wants to arrive home to an unmade bed or dishes stacked high in the sink, no one wants to show up in the morning to a chaotic, poorly tended workplace.

I believe in order not just in my and my employees' offices, but also in the common areas of our workplace, including our shared kitchen and bathroom. It's not just a matter of common courtesy; it goes deeper than that. From your business logo to the flowers blooming in the entrance, maintaining an all-around impression of cleanliness, efficiency, and professionalism has a potent effect on how we perceive ourselves and how our clients perceive us.

(For evidence of the Swiss-watch workplace in action, see the Office Gallery.)

All Together Now

If your office has a conference room, make sure you run it and maintain it as precisely as you do the rest of your workplace. Conference rooms should always be booked in advance, since nothing could be worse than eighteen people converging at the same time in a room that has space for twelve. Before a scheduled meeting, make sure everything is in place, and when the meeting is over, a staff member should return the room to its default condition: tidy, functional, and ready for the next powwow.

I always like to provide conference room visitors with the niceties they might find if they were visiting my home (with the exception of a Tempur-Pedic mattress, of course). I make it a point to have preset at every seat a pad of paper and pen and a glass or bottle of water ready to be poured, along with a cocktail napkin with my business logo printed on it. On a side table or counter, I'll set out an ice bucket and a bowl of nuts. As usual, we offer everyone tea or coffee.

If the meeting is taking place in my personal office, I have an extra pad of paper and pen available and will always offer my visitors a beverage and a snack. No exceptions!

Desk Etiquette

A clean desk is an important component of the overall Swiss-watch effect of an office, and goes a long way toward creating an across-the-board environment of professionalism and efficiency.

The surface of your desk should be free of any clutter, and that includes family photographs. (Much as I love family, a desk shouldn't resemble a shrine to nieces, nephews, aunts, uncles, and your spunky, river-rafting great-grandmother Louise!) The wastebasket shouldn't be overflowing with used coffee cups or, for that matter, with anything. If you have a computer in your office, select a screen saver that won't offend anyone and, preferably, shows off the company's logo.

This same tidiness and attention to detail should continue inside the drawers. Clearly organize and label the contents of each. If you keep folders inside the drawers, make sure they're labeled so you can locate them at a moment's notice. I keep my files divided into sections, such as Big Picture, Small Picture, Day-to-Day, and Pending—the right one is at my fingertips.

When the workday is over, employees should clean stray papers and rogue pencils off their desks before shutting off the overhead lights, rolling their chairs back under their desks, and drawing the window blinds. Good night, and see you in the morning!

Time I$ Energy: It's Later than You Think

I remember reading a story once about an extremely successful executive. He attributed his success to a technique that allowed him to get more work done daily than most of his colleagues managed to accomplish in a whole week. Simple to understand though admittedly not all that simple to execute, his philosophy can be boiled down to this: He makes it a rule never to deal with a piece of paper, e-mail, or individual task more than once. He reads his e-mail in the order in which it comes in, and answers incoming e-mail instantly instead of putting it off. If the document he's reading demands an immediate reply, he'll jump right to it. He handles his to-do list the same way, crossing off as much as possible as soon as possible, and not putting off the difficult tasks for later or sweeping them under the rug. Correctly, he believes that it's a monumental waste of time to reread (and delay attending to) e-mail, documents, or papers that he's already read once.

If you're a scanner (as I used to be and am still sometimes guilty of being), you've most likely read several e-mail messages in your inbox multiple times. With this new method of dealing with them right away, however, I find that my inbox is virtually empty. I ruthlessly move down the list, checking off one, then another—done!—then deleting them. Try it yourself. I promise your efficiency will shoot through the roof! (Granted, every now and then when you get a twenty-page legal document, you'll have to set it aside until you have the time to address it.)

Who You Are: Logos and Letterheads

Every business has its own individual style. Some workplaces are casually snazzy, some traditionally corporate, others as buttoned up and formal as a black-tie event at the Metropolitan Museum. Whatever your workplace style, any and all written business communications should reflect your company's image and philosophy. Your style and logo should be consistent and uniform. If you're known for

You Have Three Seconds to Make a First Impression

First impressions are absolutely vital. They can make the difference between a client who feels welcome and stays, and one who has instant doubts (and could potentially make a dash for the door!). That's why I keep a system in place for whenever my employees greet workplace visitors.

First of all, if there is a conference call involving several parties, locations, and an access code, a member of my staff will make sure the line is confirmed and tested before any visitors' arrival. If the meetings are being held face to face, my employees greet our visitors politely by initiating eye contact, introducing themselves, and shaking the guests' hands firmly. They then escort visitors to the conference room or waiting area before offering to hang their coats in the closet.

The next step is so ingrained in our offices that it comes as an automatic reflex! Employees immediately offer visitors the choice of a hot or cold beverage, then deliver the beverage in a glass, on a tray, with a coaster or a cocktail napkin. Unless the boss or employee comes out to greet his or her visitors, employees should escort them to the necessary office or waiting area, then quietly vanish. They also let visitors know as soon as possible if the person they are to meet is detained, because a guest stuck in the corner and ignored will quickly become—justifiably—crabby and resentful. (As an FYI, it's rude to keep visitors with an appointment waiting longer than five minutes.)

high style and chic, make sure the calligraphy smacks of the same elements. If you're an antique dealer trafficking in centuries-old prints, modern typography just won't do! (As an added FYI, don't forget to have your name, contact address, e-mail address, and telephone number on every single piece of letterhead.)

Eat, Drink, and Be Mindful

All shared common areas, from the kitchen to the fridge to the bathroom, should maintain the same high standards as the rest of the workplace. Unfortunately, there are always a few offenders in every workplace. It's better to clean up for others if they can't take care of themselves rather than leave the kitchen or bathroom untidy for the next person. Of course, if you know who the culprit is, say something to that person. If the behavior can't be helped because the offender is, frankly, an all-around mess, then slip a note to his or her superior. You'll see how quickly he or she will improve when it is clear that the rest of the staff won't tolerate the lack of manners.

- All fridge food should live inside sealed, labeled containers. At the end of each day, the refrigerator should be cleaned out so that it looks absolutely immaculate.

- The office bathroom rivals my bathrooms at home when it comes to order and cleanliness. When they're done washing their hands, employees should wipe down any spills so the sink looks neat for the next person. (Men: Remember to put the toilet seat down when you're finished.) All employees should avail themselves of the air freshener when necessary. In short, leave it as you would like to find it.

Who's the Boss? The Proper Care and Handling of Staff

An ideal employee is eager to turn in the best possible results; has an infectiously great attitude; is happy to participate in the spirit, energy, and success of a business; understands the enormous power of first impressions; and most of all, brings to work that extra 20 percent that I define as pure *passion.* In any workplace environment, the staff tends to adopt the attitude of the person in charge. If that person is you, make sure you embody all these characteristics and more. Your staff will follow in your footsteps, and I promise that your business will be everything you've ever dreamed of.

Getting to Know You: The Job Interview

Americans are well known for writing the most compelling, amazing résumés on earth! Assume that prospective employees are willing to tell you anything, and interview them accordingly. Take advantage of referrals and recommendations, and for each position, always interview at least three to five people, which will give you a good range of choices. Double-check a person's skills, even to the extent of having him or her demonstrate the ability to draft a letter or his or her mastery of the latest office computer program. Next, consider establishing a trial period so that you and your employee can both decide if the job is the right fit. As always, make your expectations, including salary, benefits, bonuses, vacation and sick time, absolutely clear from the beginning.

During the actual interview, your manner should be friendly, but don't waste precious time engaging in small talk about the weather, the Pittsburgh Steelers, or how you feel about meringues in general. If you plan on taking notes during the interview, mention this right off the bat. Make it clear to the candidate that you plan to treat all information uttered and taken down in your office in the utmost confidence. Never forget what an interview is all about: uncovering as much as possible about the candidate's goals, aspirations, personality, and work ethic, and most important, finding the best person for the job. Don't be shy about asking personal questions as long as they relate to a candidate's ability to do his or her job: whether he or she is in a relationship, has children, and is free to travel. It's better to know these things in advance rather than find them out later.

Working Assets: Your Team

I'm a great believer in giving my team some degree of autonomy—but not before they've absorbed our office's culture of

The Twenty Most Revealing Interview Questions
1. Why are you leaving your present job?
2. What have you been criticized for during the last four years? Did you agree or disagree? Why or why not?
3. Describe the most ideal—and the least ideal—boss you could choose.
4. What activities in your current position do you enjoy the most?
5. What activities do you enjoy the least?
6. How do you criticize your subordinates?
7. What would you do if you detected a peer falsifying expense records?
8. How would you describe your management style (if applicable)? How would you describe your old boss's management style?
9. If you had a choice, would you rather draw up plans or implement them?
10. Describe one or two situations in which you did not succeed, and explain why. (You can learn the most from "failure" stories, and how the employee resolved the situation.)
11. What do you think determines an individual's progress most often in a successful firm?
12. How would you deal with a pressure-cooker situation where you're faced with multiple deadlines and a shortage of time?
13. Describe your most unpleasant work experiences.
14. In your current job, what problems have you identified that were previously overlooked?
15. What work improvements have you instigated in other jobs?
16. What methods are most effective in dealing with people?
17. What methods are least effective?
18. What's the most useful piece of criticism you've ever received?
19. What about the most useless?
20. How do you plan a day's work?

Suggestion: If you like the candidate generally and can't make up your mind, I suggest walking him or her to his car after the interview. If the candidate has weeds growing out of the glove compartment and a week's laundry in the backseat, it's a fairly clear indication of how his or her desk is going to look! No car? Eye (but don't rifle through!) the employee's purse or briefcase.

"Sometimes when we hire people, we get great hardware . . . but the software is not always installed. As the employer, it's your responsibility to keep the most current software operating and running at 120 miles an hour. If you hire well, you won't have to fire!"

pride, efficiency, and professionalism. Naturally, I micromanage all new employees, but as time goes on and members of my staff travel around the world with me, and demonstrate that they know how to get the job done to their own high standards, and mine, I give them additional freedoms and responsibilities. However, creatively—*always*—I'm hands-on, and in charge.

Positive Reinforcement

I'm a huge believer in giving compliments wherever and whenever they're deserved. My staff is loyal to me because I treat them the same way I would wish to be treated: with graciousness, respect, and fairness. I never forget to acknowledge the amazing efforts they put in every single day. If employers behave with humility, and treat others the same way, it's astounding how much respect they'll receive in return. You'll be surprised and even amazed by how much simple acknowledgment equates to increased productivity. What you give out in a spirit of generosity comes back to you tenfold! Just as I'm someone who doesn't relish being berated or screamed at, you'll never catch me having a Russell Crowe moment and hurling phones against the wall. For me, a surefire way to motivate my employees is to appreciate their best work honestly, sincerely, and often, resisting the very human temptation to find fault and finger-point, and reserve whatever criticisms I might have until an appropriate time. I never start with a negative. Rather, I find the good in whatever's been done, then circle back to what could be improved. By the time we discuss what needs changing, my staff is only too happy to oblige and will make the effort to fix any problems.

Example: I show up at one of my party or wedding sites and find that a tent or a stage hasn't been draped the way I want, and it will have to be redone (usually with lots of blood, sweat, tears, and a scarily looming deadline). Faced with this situation—which is common in the events business, sadly—a lot of bosses lose their cool, yelling and carrying on, blaming everyone from the construction workers to the on-site manager. It instantaneously turns the entire workplace sour. Employees *will* excel if they're encouraged and rewarded—

and screaming at someone has precisely the opposite effect. As their leader, the aim in my business is to get the results we need. Therefore, it's more important to figure out what went wrong, how it can be fixed, and how we can make sure it never happens again.

Thus, I'll make it a priority to list a few things the crew has done that look absolutely spectacular. Only then will I suggest that the tent or fountain needs an adjustment—and then I'll explain that the members of my crew are the only people who can help me fix it. The response I get 99 percent of the time will be: "No problem, Colin." The result: precisely what I want —and a staff (and a boss) whose loyalty has been honored and rewarded.

The Power of an Immediate Apology

To me, saying "I'm sorry" (and actually meaning it) is one of the best and quickest ways I know of to defuse and disarm a situation. It is among the most valuable tools I use, whether I'm at home, in the workplace, or traveling. It takes less than ten seconds. It clears the air like a late-afternoon shower. It signals to another person that you understand his or her viewpoint, and you acknowledge that your own viewpoint maybe wasn't the best one at the time. It helps everybody move forward.

Saying "I'm sorry" isn't necessarily about who's right and who's wrong. It's about taking responsibility for a situation that is threatening to spill out of control. You can defuse most small misunderstandings with an immediate apology. On the other hand, I've found that if you have a larger dispute or disagreement with anyone, from a colleague to a spouse to a live-in partner, there is no use poisoning a situation with uncontrolled emotion. Instead, wait a day or two, and you'll find you may approach the source of the problem differently. If I'm upset at someone, I might wait four or five days before bringing up the subject again. By then, our tempers have cooled down, and both our egos are willing to revisit the source of the argument in a more reasonable way.

Make sure you understand the difference between an apology that's sincere and one that's insincere. Are you saying

"I'm sorry" because you actually feel remorseful? Check your intentions, and if they're pure, issue an apology from the heart: "I'm very sorry I messed up. The last thing I ever want to do is upset you, and I will make sure this *never* happens again."

The Rewards Program

Members of a dedicated staff tend to put in long hours and frequently give up their weekends, too. I consider it essential to reward committed employees for their amazing efforts. If a couple members of your team haven't slept for days while putting the finishing touches on a crucial project, give them a Friday off. At vacation time, take them by surprise by presenting them with a bonus. Or if you have frequent flyer miles saved up, consider allocating some of them to star employees as a year-end reward—a long weekend in Montserrat, anyone? If you have a particular division that is very profitable and all of its staff members work incredibly hard, incentivize them by sharing a portion of the profits on a quarterly or annual basis. You'll be surprised how hard your staff will work when their efforts end up in their pockets.

And remember that people don't exclusively want monetary rewards. Praise and appreciation for hard work well done are a must along the way!

She (or He) Is Me

Your assistant is an extension—and an expression—of you and the way you are perceived. Therefore, speak to him or her as you yourself would like to be spoken to. "Please" should come before every request, and "Thank you" should follow every gesture; both go a long way toward motivating staff members. Be absolutely clear as to what you expect, how and when your assistant should present his or her work, how you like to have your telephone answered, when to take a message and when to track you down, and who's on your priority phone list. If you have a request that falls outside the parameters of your assistant's job description (ordering lunch, picking up a gift), make sure you put it in the form of a polite request, and not just a blunt, "I need my dry cleaning, stat."

The Talk Cure

Look out for, and protect, the people who work with you, and they'll do the same in return. Make sure you check in with employees on a regular basis. Weekly or monthly, summon your team for a roundtable discussion that you emcee yourself. Set an agenda so all team players can participate. Get problems and frustrations out in the open. Make a point of admitting fault first in any given situation. *Never* leave a meeting without a next-steps plan of action and a clear delineation of who is doing what, so the project can move forward in the interim!

Kid Stuff

My advice is always to be flexible when it comes to female employees with children. If employees call in with a child-care crisis, I'm happy to let them work from home as long as they produce the results we're both after. In the end, it's far more important to measure a job well done than it is to be completely unrealistic about form.

Shh!

Wherever possible, do your best to maintain the tightest possible divisions between your personal and your professional life. It's easy to allow your employees to get enmeshed in your nonwork life. They'll want to please you and get to know your every like, dislike, favorite kind of chocolate, and even the brand of veal-flavored treats your dog loves. But never forget who's in charge—and who's not—and keeping your personal life out of the office will save you from blurry boundaries and overstepping employees. I find that very few people—either employees or employers—understand boundaries. Bosses should clearly establish (and guard) what's in and what's out of bounds. Most of my employees are also my social friends. I've made it clear to them all that working hours are for work, and after hours are for play. Nicknames, inside jokes, and words of affection blur the work/play line and should be strictly reserved for after hours.

Just as the boss should keep his or her personal life private, so should employees. If something is wrong at home, but it's not affecting your work, your boss really doesn't need to know the particulars. If, however, your personal problems are adversely affecting your work, then explain the situation in a straightforward manner, as well as any possible solutions you've come up with to deal with the issue at hand. Your boss will appreciate your candor.

Daily Decorum for Employers
To Whom It May Concern

How can you choose the right person to write you a recommendation? Choose someone who knows your work well, someone who has seen you take on additional responsibilities (and remain cool as a cucumber), or someone who has seen you meet improbable challenges with grace, passion, and excellence. Failing that, choose someone with whom you feel you have the best working relationship, or who knows your work inside and out.

Advice for the Job Applicant: The Brand Is You

We've looked at the workplace from the boss's point of view. But what about the potential employee's? If you're interviewing for a job, it's crucial to think of yourself as a marketable commodity. You're selling a fabulous new product—yourself —and don't forget it!

How Do I Get the Job?

Try to make a confident, energetic first impression at your job interview. Don't be overdressed or arrive wearing an outfit so flamboyantly sexy that you seem to be looking for a new husband, not a job. Find a middle ground that also manages to express your individuality—a pair of fabulous, knockout shoes never hurts! Men should wear a well-tailored suit or a jacket and pressed pants, clean shoes, and an unflashy tie. The most important thing is to look neat, clean, wrinkle-free, and pulled together. If you have any doubts at all about your appearance, glance at yourself in the bathroom mirror beforehand. Ask yourself: "Is this the best possible way I can sell myself? Will my employer consider me an addition to his or her business?" If the answer is no, edit quickly and don't be late or too early for the interview!

Presentation Is Everything

Greet your potential employer with a firm handshake, and maintain direct eye contact as much as possible. Don't forget that great posture communicates an enormous amount about a person. Ten points if you arrive looking healthy and successful and energetic; ten points off if you show up disheveled and ten minutes late, with late-night circles under your eyes and a two-day growth.

Out of Sight, But Not Out of Mind

Send a follow-up letter after the interview, thanking your potential employer and reinforcing your interest in the position (if it still interests you). It makes an efficient, elegant lasting impression and keeps you on the radar screen. If the potential employer will be making a decision quickly, an e-mail is perfectly appropriate.

Keep It Real

Make sure that your résumé is absolutely truthful. Don't put down that you speak fluent Spanish and can play all nineteen Chopin nocturnes if you can't find Mexico on a map and consider "Chopsticks" the musical equivalent of swimming to Dover.

On the Money

Don't bring up money during the job interview. That's the interviewer's job, not yours. If the subject comes up, don't squirm and exaggerate the salary you're currently earning. A simple phone call can confirm the truth, and no one wants to hire a liar straight off the bat! Also, make sure that the people you've listed as references are ready, willing, and enthusiastically able to speak for you.

Landing the Job

How to Succeed in Business by Really Trying

You've gotten the job—a big relief—and it's your first day, week, month. So how do you garner the attention and respect of your boss and colleagues?

- Add energy by smiling; by maintaining a polite, professional attitude; and by being mindful and conscious of the people who work around you. Your colleagues will love you for it, and your boss can't help but notice.

- Aim high, and you will always rise to the top.

- Never shout! There is literally no room or need for that kind of behavior. Make sure you are not the one to create that exception!

- Always acknowledge the great efforts of your colleagues.

- I believe that competition in a work environment is extremely healthy. Let the sheer power of your presentation do the work for you.

- Focus on the tasks before you, and your productivity will soar. Your boss will notice, too!

Dressing for Success

Another critical aspect of the Swiss-watch workplace: the right wardrobe. If you come to work in baggy shorts and an old Grateful Dead T-shirt, chances are you won't inspire confidence in either your coworkers or your employer. It's essential to look as professional as possible: clean, neat, ironed, and pulled together. Dress well and appropriately, but also consider adding a personal expression of individual style to your outfit. It could be a gloriously unusual belt buckle. It could be a wild scarf you picked up at a vintage store. It could be a bright red handbag. For men, it could be a colorful necktie or a nicely cut vest. Make it up! Bring something new and different to the table, and I guarantee that you'll get yourself noticed! If shorts and T-shirts are the accepted dress at

Keep Your Identity to Yourself

Identity theft takes place when someone uses your personal information —such as your Social Security number, birth date, or mother's maiden name—to impersonate you. In a lot of cases, these identity thieves will use this information to apply for loans, rent apartments, or open up new accounts with credit card companies and department stores. They then rack up hundreds—or even hundreds of thousands—of dollars in charges. Identity thieves can also use your Social Security number to get work and earn income, which will then be reported to the IRS as money *you* have earned. Though there's not all that much you can do to prevent identity theft, here are a few ways to keep your identity close to home:

- Never, ever keep sensitive, personal information on your Rolodex, on your computer, on a PDA, or on a cell phone. Keep it in a safe, tucked-away corner of your house, and keep a copy in the hands of a trusted friend or relative.

- If your wallet or purse is stolen, immediately cancel all your credit cards, and have the companies issue new ones. Next, contact all three credit-reporting agencies—Equifax, Experian, and TransUnion—and have them place a fraud alert on your account (Equifax: 800-525-6285; Experian: 800-397-3742; TransUnion: 800-680-7289). If your driver's license (or any other government-issued document) was in your wallet, contact the agencies that issued the documents and follow their procedures for cancellation and replacement. Also, ask the agency to flag your file so that no one else can use your name to obtain any additional documentation.

- Never supply your Social Security number to anyone or any business that really doesn't need it.

- When making a transaction or paying for services, keep your eye on your credit card whenever possible. Thieves could scan your card or photograph the front of it and e-mail the number to someone waiting to make transactions on your card before you can get back to your car or your home.

- Shred documents you consider too sensitive to go into the trash or a paper-recycling pile. These include all unsolicited, preapproved credit card offers.

- Make sure your computer is outfitted with firewall and antivirus software, and make sure you keep these applications up to date.

"One of my biggest pet peeves is when someone has an assistant place a call, get me on the line, . . . and then put me on hold! If your assistant places your calls for you, make sure you're on the line when the recipient picks up. No one's time is more important than anyone else's!"

your office, they should still be clean and ironed, just as if a suit were de rigueur!

Give Good Phone!

Both bosses and employees should greet telephone callers with a warm and friendly manner, followed by an introduction: "Good morning, this is Juliet Dickey. How may I help you?" Avoid answering the phone when you're in a hellish mood, or just after an argument with a colleague, or right after you've gotten a paper cut, a court summons, or had a bad oyster. Responding when grumpy often leads to poisoning and may even sabotage your next few encounters.

When calling someone for the first time, show respect by using courtesy titles. Example: "Hello, this is Colin Cowie calling. May I please speak with *Ms.* Zamor?" I dislike complete strangers addressing me on the telephone by my first name. I feel it's my prerogative to say, either immediately or at some point in the conversation, "Oh, please call me Colin." If you make a call and recognize the person answering the phone, or the person introducing himself or herself to you, by all means acknowledge this. "Hello, Mrs. Zamor, this is Colin Cowie calling. May I please speak with Ms. Zamor?"

When dealing with prominent people—or people who may be household names—always address them by their last names. Should they request otherwise, then by all means indulge your excitement and do so!

The Next Voice You Hear

Your outgoing voice-mail message should be warm, friendly, clear, and succinct.

The Right Message

When you're leaving a message on someone's voice mail, be clear and specific, state your first and last name, speak slowly, and make sure you include all the necessary details. Example: "Charles, I'm sorry we haven't been able to connect. I'd like to speak with you tomorrow, Thursday, the twenty-second, at ten A.M. eastern time, to review the materials you sent to my attention. Please call me at 212-555-1212, or e-mail me confirmation that ten A.M. works for you." If you're leaving a phone number, don't rattle it off at the speed of sound!

When leaving a message with an assistant, giving your name, your reason for calling, and what you need is perfectly sufficient. If my message is lengthy and needs immediate attention, I always request an e-mail address as well. Better that you write exactly what you need rather than relaying it to a third party or leaving a verbal dissertation. Before hanging up, always have the assistant repeat your name and telephone number for the sake of verification.

The Golden Retriever

If you're out of town, or especially snowed under with work, have someone from your office return voice-mail messages by calling to say that you're traveling or in meetings. Have your assistant—of if you don't have an assistant, a trusted coworker (lunch the next day is on you, or you cover for her the next time)—find out whether the call is urgent or if it can wait until you return to the office. Schedule phone dates. Instead of playing phone tag, leave a message, voice mail, or e-mail to set up a phone call at a specific time. If you have an appointment downtown, and you're uptown, by all means schedule a call on your cell phone while you're in transit.

Person-to-Personally

If you need to make a doctor's appointment or call in a grocery order, fine. But don't plan your entire wedding from the office, or arrange for your pet's play dates. In short, don't abuse office hours for all your personal needs and projects—and that includes instant messaging and e-mailing friends (except during your lunch hour)! And you should not use the office as the nearest post office for packages that you mail off to family and friends. If you do need to make long-distance calls, use an 800 calling number billable to your home phone (many companies monitor this type of activity via phone and e-mail records).

In the same vein, be careful with all business correspondence. Without giving in to wild paranoia, assume that somewhere, someone is monitoring it. If your message is confidential, don't use your work e-mail unless it's absolutely necessary.

A few other basic guidelines to great time management:

- Skip all the forwarded, incoming jokes (most are inane and not worth your time).

- Don't read e-mails from a sender whose e-mail address you don't recognize. The risk of viruses is too great.

- Take care not to mis-send e-mail or copy an e-mail to the wrong person (the stuff of nightmares!). Send copies only to people who *really* need to know. If you don't waste your colleagues' time, chances are they won't waste yours.

- Keep meticulous, clearly labeled records. Create a folder in your mail program or on your desktop where you store all correspondence. If you need a paper trail, print out e-mails and place them in the proper folder.

The Walls Have Ears

Whether or not you've signed a confidentiality agreement, as an employee you should assume that anything you hear during office hours stays in the office under lock and key. The only way to protect yourself from being blamed for saying something you shouldn't have said is not to say anything at all.

He Said, She Said: Dodging Office Politics

In some offices, it's inevitable. An employee plays one colleague against another, a rumor starts, and before long your workplace is a snake pit of hurt feelings, betrayals, private conversations, across-the-room glares, and lost productivity. Think high school, but without the cheerleaders and pom-poms.

Office politics can undo the success and camaraderie of an entire organization. The best way to avoid falling into the office-politics trap is to mind your own business! If someone tells you something in confidence, keep it to yourself. In my personal experience, as the boss, nine times out of ten, a rumor will make its way back to me. In these situations, my philosophy is to approach the source of the rumor and nip it in the bud at once rather than allow it to poison the energy of the work environment. If an employee hears a rumor that could be damaging to the company, he or she should tell the boss, quietly, and at once.

In Vino Disastrous

Be on your best behavior at office holiday parties (that means a two-drink maximum). Many have found out the hard way that alcohol is the ultimate truth serum. I love love just as much as the next person, but hearing an employee slur "I l-e-r-v-e you sooooo, sooooo much" leaves me a little cold. No one *really* wants to become the newest office scandal—and no one wants to witness it!

Sexual Harassment

Sexual harassment is epidemic in today's corporate culture, and it can range from off-color jokes to leering to subtle demands for sex in exchange for career promotion, all of which lead to an overall hostile work environment. It's also against the law, as is retaliating against someone who has made a complaint of sexual harassment.

I personally make it a point never to touch an employee for any reason whatsoever in my workplace. As the boss, I'm also legally responsible to "take reasonable care" to prevent, stop, and properly correct any instances of sexual harassment committed by my employees. This not only involves distributing to employees our policy spelling out company-wide prohibitions against sexual harassment, but also enforcing it and investigating any accusations. Make absolutely sure you do the same!

Sexual harassment must be severe or pervasive for it to meet the legal definition. If you're an employee, avoid making comments about a coworker's clothing, personal behavior, or physical appearance; don't tell jokes of a sexual nature, or pursue a colleague romantically; never touch a person inappropriately or send him or her suggestive e-mails, drawings, or pictures. If you're an employee who feels you're being sexually harassed, it's important that you say no to the offender clearly, keep a paper trail, inform your boss, and if need be, file a discrimination complaint with the Equal Employment Opportunity Commission and/or your state's fair employment agency.

Through the Fire: Letting an Employee Go: Five Guidelines

Sometimes an employee you've hired simply doesn't work out. The workload is too great, they've betrayed your trust, they interviewed far better than they perform, or you're generally dissatisfied with the quality of their work. If someone has committed a workplace crime or stolen from you, that's one thing, and that person should be let go the day before yesterday. But dismissing an employee for performance problems should be handled with finesse and diplomacy.

1. Every good employee deserves a dignified exit. If you're dismissing an employee, fire them so they leave (if possible) still loving you, or at least respecting you (see below). It's also better for everyone—the employee, the boss, and the rest of your staff—if the employee who's been let go leaves immediately. No one wants the unspoken tension of working side by side with someone who's just been told he or she has two weeks to clean out his or her desk.

2. If I'm letting someone go, I will first speak to my security and technology people to make sure that they alter any personal information, such as computer passwords and e-mail access. Better safe than sorry.

3. Always dismiss an employee with dignity. All of us have heard horror stories of employees being escorted out by a poker-faced security man, or arriving at work to find their office door padlocked, or being told by phone, "Your services are no longer required here." Unless your employee is a felon, this is both unnecessary and graceless.

bosses

If someone asks you to supply a reference, be extremely careful what you write. If you suggest that an employee has been dishonest or otherwise larcenous (and guilty), you'd better be able to defend that position in a potential lawsuit! If asked about the integrity of an employee you've suspected of dishonesty, it's always better to say, "I'd rather not talk about that." Without incriminating yourself, you can get the message across. But most potential new employers can easily spot the difference between "He was pleasant, punctual, and did his work well" and "He has honesty and integrity, was dedicated to his work, and will be hugely missed around here."

4. I'll bring the person into my office, sit him or her down, and say something like, "I wish that I had a better way of doing this, but I'm changing direction with the company, and I don't really see a spot for you here anymore. You're welcome to leave right now, or at the end of the week with two weeks' severance pay." Sometimes, depending on the terms of the employee's contract, I will also offer a bonus or exit package, but generally it's on a case-by-case basis.

5. Have your lawyer write up a bullet-proof dismissal agreement in writing, outlining the terms of dismissal; the severance package, including any bonuses, exit packages, or unused vacation time owed the employee; as well as a clause that forfeits the employee's right to sue you for wrongful termination. Have your employee sign it in exchange for an agreed-upon severance payment, and then both of you can move forward.

Working at Home: The Basics

Thanks to computers, e-mail, cell phones, and all the other conveniences of modern communication, more and more employees are able to work out of their houses and apartments and bypass a faraway office or distant city entirely. The home office arrangement may seem ideal, and it can be, too, under the right circumstances. Here are a few definite things to keep in mind:

- Separate church and state! If at all possible, your home office should be physically and psychologically removed from your living quarters, from rooms that you normally associate with leisure, relaxation, and pure fun. Otherwise, you're setting yourself up for a scenario of work, work, work all the time, and who needs that? Technology will become an irresistible allure, and possibly an addiction. It's far too tempting to sneak away from dinner or a cozy evening with your family to cast one final look at your e-mail inbox or your BlackBerry. Alternatively, many people who work at home are faced with nontechnological distractions: that comfy bed over there for a quick nap, the kitchen for whipping up a quick smoothie. There's nothing wrong with returning to the office at night before retiring for bed to do a quick e-mail check, or preparing a midday sandwich—just make sure that overall you do your best to maintain the boundaries between the personal and the professional.

- Create divisions and structure, both within the physical space of your home or apartment and within your own head. Decide what time you're going to go to your office, and what time you're going to call it quits for the day. Then stick to it! Eight hours a day is more than enough to get everything done. Any longer, and your efficiency wanes.

- Maintain order. A clean, well-organized office will make you feel in control of your life, and save you hours of digging through drawers in search of a pen, a cell phone recharger, or a box of paper clips. Which brings me to the next point . . .

- Keep your home office well stocked! You can save time, energy, and emergency trips to the computer store by making sure you have more than enough of everything you need at all times (tip: buy online for efficiency).

- Set up a separate telephone line so that after 6:00 P.M. you'll know whether there's a client on the line or one of your friends. You can also address this confusion by programming separate rings on the same telephone.

- It's important to create good everyday habits and to adhere to high standards of personal and professional discipline. Get your exercise out of the way in the morning, then shower, dress, and "go to the office." At the end of the day, turn down the ringer on the office line. Physically "leave" the office for the day—then sink into the comfort of your home!

six

traveling in style: surrender to the journey

The days of high-glam air travel are a thing of the long-ago past. Airports are busier than ever; gates miles apart; flights delayed, canceled, or overbooked; and the airlines are bordering on bankruptcy. That doesn't mean we have to abandon our goal of living chicly when we fly.

I spend much of the year on the road, traveling from one event and hot spot to another. After flying literally millions of miles (six million with American Airlines alone!), I've learned a lot about how to deal with heightened security measures, skeleton crews, and a steep decrease in basic good service. Wherever I'm traveling, my philosophy is always the same: simplicity, efficiency, ease. And most important: surrender.

Whether I'm stuck in an airport or a traffic jam, my travel mantra bears repeating: *surrender.* I give up all illusion of control. I let go, and go forward. Instead of trying in vain to achieve perfection, I do what I can to cooperate with the long lines and inconveniences around me.

It wasn't always that way. I used to be the most irate, frazzled traveler on the planet until it finally hit me: We may be the pilots of our own lives, but travel today is one aspect of life in which we must give up control to the moment-by-moment stresses. As you know well, no doubt, that means potential delays, irritating lines, lost luggage lunacy, and the other inconveniences of getting from one place to another.

It's no use fighting, so I try to go with the flow. I no longer allow an extra few hours to cause me grief. Whether it's a short two-hour drive or a long overnight red-eye, I write off my travel days and use the wait time to be productive with my laptop or reading material. Or I use the time to place phone calls. If I've decided to spend the time relaxing instead, I just breathe in deeply, exhale slowly, and take a moment to say a short prayer asking my Higher Power to deliver me in one piece as quickly and efficiently as possible. Any added comfort is a bonus!

There are three elements to graceful travel: planning ahead, being considerate of people along the way, and reducing stress. From packing my bags to leaving on a jet plane to touching down in a faraway destination, this chapter contains the tricks and techniques I've picked up along the way.

Know Before You Go

As soon as you know you are traveling, make your reservations. Specify the type of room you want. Ask what views your hotel has. Is there a park you'd like to face? Avoid any hotel room close to an elevator (noise) or kitchen (smells) or overlooking the parking lot! Ask if they have smoke-free floors. Just before your departure, check the local weather on the Internet, or call the hotel concierge and introduce yourself. The concierge will tell you whether it's sunny or bone chilling, and help you do anything that requires advance reservations. If you're on a honeymoon, let him know so that the hotel can go out of its way to make your stay special.

Suggestion: The concierge deals with guests' needs and makes reservations. The general manager runs the hotel. Discuss arrangements with the concierge, hotel problems with the general manager. (See my tipping primer on pages 234–37.)

Reservation Tips

Rather than just calling the airlines and saying, "Book it," here are some simple guidelines to follow when you're making your next reservation:

- What type of equipment will you be flying? Ask for the seat configuration.

- Select an aisle or a window so you're not stuck claustrophobically between Chatty Cathy and the guy who appears to be in the final stages of tuberculosis.

- Seats in the exit aisle and the bulkhead have more legroom, but often don't recline all the way. The same no-recline problem is true for the last row of any class.

- Ask for a seat as close to the front as possible for an easy exit.

- First-class seats in the first row have no room to stow a computer or handbag, since there is no seat in front of you. The second row is my favorite!

- Ask ahead about meal choices. But know that starvation may well end up being the result of relying on airline food. Instead, bring your own. (See page 228 for more information.)

- If you're connecting with another flight, the reservation clerk may not inform you of other airline options that might be more convenient. Ask what other airlines provide service to your destination.

- Shop for the best fare, but do whatever you can to avoid waiting in long airport lines to pick up tickets. Most airlines have e-tickets. Take advantage of them.

- Leave a reliable contact number or mobile phone number with the airline. If any of your flights have been canceled or rerouted or otherwise delayed, the airline will do its best to call to inform you. Check your voice mail! If your flight is delayed, booking a second or even third backup

reservation is wise advice given today's security concerns. Better yet, while you are waiting for an update regarding your delay, call your travel agent and start your backup plan right away, because the moment the airline makes that announcement, three hundred other people will be doing the same thing. If you didn't use a travel agent in the first place, use a PDA, BlackBerry, or airport wireless zone to access your online travel provider.

- An excellent travel agent is worth his or her weight in gold. Drop a postcard, propose marriage, offer a kidney to him or her if you can spare one—this is one relationship worth cultivating! I always send my travel agent notes and feedback on a new hotel or destination. This way she better understands my needs and likes and will suggest and custom-book more knowingly for me next time around.

Packing Smartly: Carry On!

If you pack smartly, you'll feel smart, organized, and put together. Knowing that all the possessions you're traveling with are in a certain place relieves a lot of anxiety. You may even find that having smart-looking luggage inspires you to be more organized. I collect black pieces because black travels well and always looks stylish. Today you can choose between countless beautifully designed luggage pieces in gorgeous leathers and high-tech materials, sized for overhead compartments and outfitted with wheels for those epic treks from airport gate to boarding gate that would otherwise require yaks and sherpas. Well-made carry-ons, laptop bags, and totes make the difference between maintaining your sanity and having a meltdown in that middle distance between home and destination.

Inside my carry-on bag, I pack all the things I cannot live without for twenty-four hours (or more), including:

- My laptop computer.

- The cables for my computer, my iPod, iPod charger and headphones, and my cell phone charger. I keep all these cables in a small bag. Each cord is wound up and secured with a rubber band. This saves me hours of untangling cords and figuring out which goes where when I'm looking for something or unpacking.

- My ever-ready, prepacked toiletries bag, which contains a toothbrush, dental floss, a comb, a brush, and three-ounce bottles and tubes of toothpaste, shampoo, facial scrub, facial cleanser, moisturizer, and small supplies of Tylenol, Ambien, and Airborne. I never, ever unpack this bag, so it's always ready for my next flight. And on those extremely rare occasions when I check luggage, such as when I travel home to Africa at Christmas for two weeks, I always carry the bag of essentials with me in the carry-on luggage.

- Books and magazines.

- A plastic travel folio containing my passport and driver's license; a copy of my itinerary with the name of my hotel and its phone and fax numbers; confirmation numbers for all my flights, cars, and hotels; the phone number of the car service if I've arranged for one on the other end, and all my health and life insurance data. That way, I have in my possession a single document with every bit of information I need. Before leaving my apartment, I make a copy of my passport and several copies of the rest of my itinerary. One copy goes to my office, so my colleagues will know where I can be reached every minute of the day and night, and the original stays with me.

- Several business cards, stationery, and a good pen, so I can catch up on any handwritten correspondence or thank-you notes.

- A few ten-dollar bills and a bunch of fives and ones for tipping.

- One or two unwrapped gifts (a beautifully boxed fragrant candle, incense) in case someone invites me into his or her home or for use in my hotel room.

ATM cards work almost everywhere and typically give you a better exchange rate than travelers' checks.

- Disinfectant wipes to wipe down the dining tray and arm-rests (sometimes even the seat of the plane) and antibacterial hand soap.

- A comfortable neck pillow.

- A lightweight blanket and a pashmina for use as a neck roll, a scarf, or even as a blanket.

Suggestion: Don't pack anything in your check-through luggage you'd mind losing terribly much. Keep any jewelry, medicine, camera equipment, clean underwear, and anything else you need and can't live without for a day or two in your carry-on bag.

Locked and Loaded: Checked Luggage Basics

As a man who's traveled around the globe more times than he can count, I've picked up a few fail-safe packing techniques along the way:

- Efficiency is everything! I make every possible effort to get where I'm going with only carry-on luggage. That way, I avoid the chaos of checking luggage at my point of origin, and dealing with its very slow return on the luggage carousel when I arrive at my destination.

- I try not to bring anything with me that's not absolutely essential to my trip. Naturally, this involves reviewing my schedule thoroughly beforehand and making the necessary edits and tweaks. If I know that formal black tie is needed for an upcoming weekend event, I will FedEx my outfit to the destination ahead of time so it's waiting for me in the hotel room when I get there (depending on the hotel where I'm staying, I'll either call the concierge beforehand if I need it ironed or pressed, or request an ironing board and do it myself). Even better, I can use the same box my tuxedo came in to ship it back home once I'm done.

- Wherever I'm traveling, I bring with me, along with socks and underwear, a couple of T-shirts, two white button-down shirts, a black turtleneck, a dark cashmere sweater, a good pair of jeans, two or three pairs of slacks—or one pair of slacks plus a suit—as well as workout gear (running shorts and a workout shirt). In short, multiple outfits that can take me from casual to more formal at a moment's notice.

- I pack all my clothes in clear-plastic, zippered envelopes—shirts in larger, separate, see-through bags, my trousers in another, and underwear, socks, and belts in another. I'll also bring along a separate clear bag for dirty laundry. This allows me to pack and unpack in a moment's notice and to see what's in the bag without obstruction. At the end of the day, I fold the clothing I've worn that's still clean and return it to the envelope. I'll fold and place my soiled clothing in another envelope. When I get home, separating what is clean, what needs to be pressed, and what needs to be hung up happens in an instant. (See the Travel Gallery.)

- If I'm bringing a suit with me, I take it out immediately when I get to my hotel room and hang it in the bathroom so that when I run a hot shower, most times the steam takes out any wrinkling or squashing the fabric may have endured during the flight.

The Best Medicine

In addition to any prescription or over-the-counter medications you might take, here are several traveling medications I swear by and consider absolutely essential. (Be sure to consult with your doctor before taking any medication, however.)

- Before boarding the plane, I swallow a single aspirin, which can help ward off deep-vein thrombosis, or ministrokes, which occur when a clot temporarily clogs an artery, and a section of the brain doesn't get the blood it needs.

- I am an ardent devotee of the immune-boosting product known as Airborne. Air travel, unfortunately, always means breathing recirculated air. So if my seatmate has the flu, I'm normally a goner, but by taking Airborne, I have a better chance of arriving on the other side with my health intact.

- I always bring along sleeping medication—Ambien, in my case—though I make sure to swallow it only after the plane is in the air and only if my flight time is greater than the sleep time induced by the pill. You never know if your flight will be delayed, and it's better to have your senses about you in the event of a last-minute rescheduling. Sleeping aids are only necessary for flights longer than six hours or if your destination has a time difference of five or more hours from your city of departure.

- I'll pack only the shoes I'll need, usually one or two pairs, plus a pair of workout shoes that lie absolutely flat in my bag. I pack my shoes in bags, with plastic, see-through windows in front, so I can easily pull what I need. Because of the space shoes take up, men should decide beforehand if they're going to go brown or black, pack the appropriate shoes, and then build their carry-on wardrobe around their decision. Because women's feet are generally smaller, they can often get away with packing more than two or three pairs.

- Naturally, both sexes should leave room in their bags for a little shopping, although out-of-state shopping can always be shipped, which can sometimes have the added benefit of saving you sales tax.

if it's tuesday, this must be belgium . . .

By changing your accessories, you can greatly increase the versatility of your clothing. Three different scarves and pairs of sunglasses can transform a single look from day to night, hip to conservative. A thin cashmere sweater in a delicious color will keep you warm on the plane or in the evenings and will add a sexy spike to your neutral-colored basics. An assortment of ties, eyeglasses, belts, bags, and shoes also provide distinctive variations.

- In some airports, security now allows you to lock your luggage, provided you use a TSA-approved lock (visit http://www.tsa.gov/travelers/airtravel/assistant/locks.shtm for information). I use "zip ties," which have been accepted worldwide (striated triangles that allow airport security to open them easily). Make sure each piece of luggage is clearly labeled with your name and address, inside and out (this includes your laptop). As an added precaution, wrap a colored ribbon around the handle of your luggage or something that will allow you to easily identify it.

I've Got a Plane to Catch!

Get your boarding passes online twenty-four hours before your flight leaves. This will save you check-in time, and if you're running late and already have your boarding pass, the airline won't give away your seat to a standby passenger.

Always call the airline or check online before you leave for the airport to determine if your flight is on time, delayed, or canceled. This can save you hours of staring into space in a crowded terminal or fighting for a place to sit or an electrical outlet for your laptop or cell phone.

No one wins in the game of last-minute airport roulette. Always leave extra time! It's better to spend half an hour calmly waiting for a flight than cursing the traffic on the free-way. Remember to factor in the unexpected. Long lines, traf-fic jams, check-in snafus, security checks, and canceled flights are all out of your control, so take the stress out of the situation by getting there early rather than arriving with moments to spare and eventually getting to your flight satu-rated with perspiration from the final sprint between gate 4 and 97.

Flights of Fancy: Comfort and Elegance

Wear comfortable but sharp-looking clothing. If there's one seat available for an upgrade to first class, they're not going to ask the person who's wearing Smurf gym shorts and an oversized purple Hard Rock Cafe sweatshirt. Don't wear tight-fitting jeans or trousers, or overalls that you'll have trou-ble unbuckling in the bathroom. You'll be sitting in almost the same position for hours, so wearing something comfortable is key.

- On the day of travel, my flying outfit can best be described as low-key chic. I wear a cotton T-shirt and a pair of soft denim jeans or black trousers, socks, and a pair of slip-on shoes or loafers that can be easily removed at the security station and when I'm in the air (no lace-up boots or shoes with buckles). If I'm wearing a belt, I wear one without a metal buckle so it can come off easily. Knowing that unpredictable temperature changes occur in the air, I bring along a soft cashmere sweater and a small, warm, easily stowable blanket or wrap.

- If I'm traveling in the winter months, I wear only dark col-ors. I find it easier to maintain a tidy, pulled-together appearance if I'm wearing black, charcoal, or navy blue.

- I never use the blankets or the pillows provided by com-mercial airlines unless they're in sealed plastic covers. Airline cleaning crews launder those blankets only once every eight flights, and frankly, that's about seven too few washings for me. I bring my own travel pillow as well.

- In the end, there is no reason to get upset at the ticket agent, jostle other travelers aside while getting on and off the plane, or complain about the food or mediocre service. What's the point? Everyone will arrive at his or her destination at the same time, the food is always terrible, and the service is invariably less than ideal. Know this, let go, and prepare for your journey as best as you can.

Airborne Manners: In-Flight

Better Take It with You

Whatever the airline is serving at thirty-eight thousand feet, it can't be that delicious, and is likely to be only passably good. In the airport, I purchase a couple of high-protein breakfast bars, bags of unsalted nuts or trail mix, a piece or two of fresh fruit, and even some cheese. If I'm leaving for the airport from my own apartment, I'll bring along something more nutritious and substantial: either a chicken breast or a homemade salad, which I place in a Ziploc bag so it's safe to pack. And if I'm leaving for the airport from a hotel, I'll ask them to prepare a fresh salad to go, with the dressing on the side. I also avoid salty food before flying. Salt causes you to retain water, and can make your feet swell. I used to take my own wine with me, but that's now out of the question!

A Tight Fit

Squeezing your luggage inside the overhead compartment is not a competitive sport! These days no one wants to check luggage, but it's completely inconsiderate to hog all the space in the cabin. Leave room for the next guy. And don't clog up the aisle while you're wrestling your luggage into the overhead; be mindful of the long line that's starting to form behind you.

On the Road Again: Traveling by Car—a Few Guidelines

- Before I leave, I always print out directions from MapQuest (http:/www.mapquest.com), though I keep travel maps in my car as well (I'm a huge fan of MapQuest, but it's worth having backup information, too).

- I check beforehand if there are any traffic delays on the routes I'll be traveling. Of course, no one can anticipate a jackknifed tractor trailer, but you *can* find out if there's a six-month-long bridge reconstruction project or a major headache-inducing detour.

- I avoid traveling during morning and evening rush hours—and pick alternate times when there'll be the fewest number of cars clogging the road.

- When I travel by car, I always bring an amenity kit. Here's what's in the glove compartment: Visine, gum, breath mints, floss, pen and pencil, lint remover, notepad, lip balm, hand cream, bottled water, and in a separate bag, CDs and magazines.

- Here's what's in the trunk: garbage bags, toilet paper (just in case), Ziploc bags, a comfy back cushion.

- I bring my own moisturizer, shampoo, and conditioner, sun block, and insect repellent.

- I make it a point to pack good cotton T-shirts. If the hotel linens are stiff, I can always place my T-shirt over the pillowcase to sleep better.

- I always bring along a cooler filled with fresh sandwiches and fruit, iced coffee or iced tea, as well as something sweet (I dare you to try to find anything remotely healthy or nutritious at a roadside fast-food stand!).

- Of course, I bring along my cell phone, as well as a cell phone recharger that plugs into my car's empty cigarette lighter. And, of course, my iPod and my iPod recharger! I wholeheartedly recommend investing in an iTrip or other gadget that permits you to play your iPod through an FM-radio station, which sets an ideal mood for whatever scenery you're driving through.

- If you hit a two-mile-long traffic jam, remember that it's out of your control. Breathe deeply—and surrender.

"And Then My Wife Left Me"

Bring magazines, a book, an iPod, or your laptop when you travel. Whether you're flying or taking the train or a bus, don't count on your seatmate for scintillating conversation or six hours' worth of solid entertainment. I consider airplane travel a part of my business, and as I mentioned, I have learned to use the time constructively. As I do when waiting, I write thank-you notes, read, work, and study. I truly enjoy being inaccessible for those hours. If you are not interested in conversation, put your earphones on; it's a fairly definite signal that you want to be left alone.

Little Timmy Wants to Organize a Hockey Game in Coach

If you are a parent traveling with children, please come prepared. Bring toys, coloring books, electronic games, and favorite foods. And please, *please* discipline your children. They may not run up and down the aisle, bang on the backs of seats, or upset other passengers while you watch the movie.

Arrive and Shine!

However many hours and time changes later, my plane has taxied to the gate and then, before I know it, I'm in the hotel lobby, checking in. Now what?

- Unless it's midnight, the first thing I do is change into my exercise clothes and have a quick workout—even if it's 6:30 A.M.! If my time is limited—say, I have to meet a client in an hour—I'll do ten to twenty minutes of floor exercises, some push-ups, sit-ups, and a few good stretches. If I have an hour or more, I'll squeeze in twenty minutes of cardio. My goal is simple: to get my blood pumping. Remember: Airline passengers have usually been dozing on the plane for the past several hours. During that time, the body's most vital organs have been at rest, too. Now is the time for a wake-up call. I've also found that exercising before a meeting gives me renewed authority and self-possession, not to mention a certain confidence. (This

All Aboard!: Train-Travel Guidelines

- Whenever I travel by train, I reserve a seat in advance. Train personnel will often overbook, and believe me, no one wants to travel while standing in an aisle, or—worse—packed in between cars!

- If for some reason I can't reserve a seat in advance, I take advantage of one of the ticket-purchasing machines in the train terminal that are similar to the ones you find in airports. They're incredibly efficient, accept all credit cards, and can save you from waiting forever in line.

- When I'm traveling by train, I take along a shopping bag filled with many of the same delicacies I bring aboard an airplane: a fresh salad, a delicious piece of grilled chicken, protein bars, fresh fruit, bottled water, and an ice pack to keep everything cold. Believe me, I'm the envy of all the other passengers!

- Nowadays, many trains offer wall sockets, so you can work away happily on your laptop as you race through cities and towns, without worrying about losing battery power. Check beforehand.

- Don't forget your iPod and headphones. If space is at a premium, and you have a chatty seatmate, placing your earphones squarely around your head will send a signal loud and clear. Though, as always, be mindful that your playlist doesn't leak out and bother the other passengers.

- I never board a train without bringing along a variety of fantastic reading materials—the novel I'm immersed in at the time, a local newspaper (preferably the *New York Post*), and an assortment of all my favorite magazines, including *Time, Vanity Fair, Town & Country, Gourmet, Bon Appétit, People,* and the not-always-easy-to-find-but-always-überdelicious *Vogue Entertaining & Travel,* Australian edition!

technique also works fantastically well before you step out onto the beach.) Stomach pulled in? Check. Color in your cheeks? Check. Vitality? Check.

- Whatever my fatigue level may be, I try to adapt to the local time zone as quickly as possible by going to bed at my usual time. If I arrive at dawn, I try to stay awake as long as humanly possible because I'm determined to be on track the next day. Sleeping pills help a lot here. I take one pill the first night, a half pill the second night, and possibly another half the third night. I repeat this formula when I return home, and my jet lag is minimal. As always, you should consult your doctor before taking any medication.

- If I'm hungry when I arrive, I'll hunt down something to eat—ideally, high-protein meals or snacks with lots of fiber. I avoid heavy carbohydrates (they tend to make me sleepier, and they clog the bowels).

- In the hotel or guest room, I make my environment feel as much as possible like home. I always bring my iPod. If for some reason I've forgotten it, my music library is on my computer, so I have familiar sounds no matter what. I bring a fragrant candle, which allows me to warm, and add spirit to, my room—not to mention hide the potential hint of smoke from the previous guest. (Note: If the room smells of smoke, you are entitled to ask the hotel to provide you with a nonsmoking room. If they don't have one, ask if they have one in a different category of room. A good hotel will give you the upgrade to keep you happy and make sure you come back.)

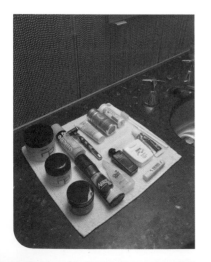

- Lastly, the bathroom. I place a washcloth or face towel on the vanity, to maintain cleanliness. Who knows how efficient the housekeeper was after the last guest? Bathroom vanities can be among the most germ-infested places on earth, no matter how talented the housekeeping staff is. I unpack and neatly place my toiletries on the towel. This little setup looks neat, it's clean, it ensures that you can find everything, and it means that there's no reason for the housekeeper to touch any of your personal things.

Hotel Hospitality Basics

If you arrive at your hotel well groomed and well mannered, I guarantee you will be treated well! Introduce yourself to the concierge and the front desk manager. If you get to your room and are unhappy, by all means call down to the front desk. Remember: If you have a complaint and are looking for an upgrade in service or accommodation, start off on a positive note. Don't threaten, yell, use vulgar language, or attract undue attention to yourself as a foreigner! Instead, say something like: "My name is Mr. Cowie. I just checked in a few minutes ago. I love the hotel, but I'm not really happy with my room. Is it possible you have something on a higher floor with a better view? Or something a bit bigger? I'll be holding a few meetings in my room, and I need space to set up an online computer presentation. How can you help me?" You'll get more attention if you're gracious than if you're demanding. Remember, many hotels keep profiles on their guests in order to make them feel more comfortable upon their return. Make sure yours doesn't have a big red flag next to it.

From my years of traveling extensively around the world and staying in all classes and types of hotels, I must say that most people in the hospitality business, when treated correctly, will go out of their way to improve your stay. If you are getting good service, then reciprocate accordingly. It's a very simple procedure. You service, I tip; or I pay and you service.

Making a Hotel Your Home Away from Home

If this is a hotel you travel to frequently, make a point of getting to know the general manager. Let him know what business you're in and what kind of work you do. If you've had a particularly pleasant stay, write a note thanking him when you get home. The next time you return, you'll probably find a bottle of wine or box of chocolates in your room to welcome you back.

The Hotel Bel Air in Los Angeles has been my home away from home for more than eighteen years. I know all the staff and they know me; they go out of their way to provide me with the best service, and I am always generous to them. And at Christmastime, don't forget to send a card or a note addressed

How to Entertain in a Hotel

Most hotels permit you to entertain in the dining room or the bar. Ask the concierge in advance to reserve a table for you and your guests. It's more thoughtful to select an appetizer, a choice of two or three entrées, and a selected dessert in advance, with a prechosen selection of wine or beverage, so that you can get down to business or entertaining right away. Once you start handing out menus and placing orders, you have already lost momentum. Take charge of the situation, and both the hotel and your guests will have the best-quality experience. An added bonus: This makes you look more efficient and put together!

On the style front, feel free to add your own place cards and flowers. Entertain in your room only if you have a suite with a separate bathroom and sitting room. Then it's appropriate to order cocktails and lunch or dinner from the hotel's room service. Prepay the check or arrange in advance to bill it to your room to avoid an awkward moment at the end of the meal.

If you're doing anything that involves press or the media, let the hotel know in advance; the management may need to give you its okay. They may upgrade you in order to showcase their own fabulous hotel, or set up a separate suite for the occasion. The more notice you give, the more prepared they will be for you!

to the staff (if you don't know the hotel well) or the general manager (if the two of you have a great professional relationship).

I always rely on the concierge. I once did a cocktail party in a foreign city in a private home. The concierge of the hotel where I was staying arranged to have the Champagne and flowers sent, made the photocopies I needed, and bought CDs. If you're polite, tip well, and acknowledge everyone's helpfulness, the concierge and entire staff will make your life a whole lot easier.

Privacy, Please

Don't hesitate to ask the hotel to screen your calls ("Miss Exhausted, I have Mr. Needy on the phone. Would you like to speak with him?"). Or you can choose to have your calls blocked completely. Though the hotel will do this automatically, for free, I believe in giving generously, so I'll often leave the desk clerk a tip of anywhere from twenty to sixty dollars, depending on the hotel.

To Ensure Prompt Service: Tips on Tipping

The world runs on gratuities! As a person who has spent a tremendous amount of time organizing and preplanning weddings, events, and other celebrations around the world, I know that money is the universal barter system. But it's often hard to know how much, or how little, to leave individual members of the service professions, whether it's a concierge in a

European hotel or the waitress from your favorite neighbor-hood restaurant.

First and foremost, it's important to remember that *tips* means "to ensure prompt service." A tip is a reward for a job carried out in a way that meets or (one can always hope!) surpasses your expectations. I err on the side of tipping gen-erously because I go into most situations anticipating fantas-tic service—and because I know that if I don't tip to secure that ocean-facing table or hard-to-get seat I'm after, some-one else *will.*

Suggestion: Hotel chain of command (in order of impor-tance) consists of the general manager, manager on duty, and front desk manager. One of these people should be able to take care of your problems. If a staff member doesn't help you, lodge a complaint with any of the above people.

In some cases, however, tipping is not appropriate. For example, there's no need to tip the airline reservations clerk who scrambled to get you on a full flight at the very last minute. Instead of a tip, I'll ask for her card and later send her a personal letter, along with a box of chocolates or a CD, something that tangibly shows my appreciation for her hard work. (As an extra bonus, nine times out of ten, when I next find myself traveling through that airport, she'll remember me with a big smile and go out of her way to be helpful.)

But in general, I believe in tipping generously and often. Whether you're lounging poolside in a Côte d'Azur hotel or hanging out at the hamburger joint down the block, I hope these guidelines will ensure prompt service!

Always tip	It's not necessary to tip
Hotel concierge	Hotel owner
Restaurant maître d'	Hotel general manager
Pool attendant	Airline reservations clerk
Waiter	Chef
Housekeeping staff	Busboy

Tipping in Hotels

I'm a huge believer in tipping up front, when I arrive or earlier, rather than afterward. If you tip someone before your arrival, then you have created an unspoken contract with that person, and believe me, everything will come your way! If you tip someone just before you leave, it naturally won't matter as much to the staff whether your stay was underwhelming.

- One of the first things I do when I arrive at a hotel is tip the hotel concierge approximately twenty dollars a day for every day of my stay. If I plan on staying five days, that comes to a hundred dollars. This may sound excessive, but the effort the concierge will then make to earn his money (and my respect) is well worth the price.

- If I'm traveling to an unfamiliar city, one where there's a limited number of truly great restaurants or sights to check out, or it's a city in which the most popular restaurants fill their reservations books quickly, I will contact the concierge well in advance to ask if there is anything I should absolutely see, hear, taste, feel, or otherwise experience in that city or region. Since the answer invariably will be yes, I'll then ask the concierge to make the necessary arrangements for me.

- Placing a call to the concierge before your arrival has the additional benefit of alerting the entire hotel staff to your visit. In most top-flight hotels, the general manager, concierge, and crew have daily and weekly meetings to discuss their upcoming arrivals. If the staff knows you're coming (and your likes and dislikes), this call automatically puts you on the hotel's radar screen!

- The best way to tip someone is to enclose the bills in a handshake or, more elegantly, to fold them in an envelope with a thank-you note. I always travel with several sheets of my own personal stationery. If you really want great attention, send a note to the concierge in advance. Enclose cash in it, introduce yourself, tell him the dates of your upcoming stay, and close with words to the effect of "I know that you are going to make our stay utterly *unbe-*

lievable for us!" When you finally arrive at the hotel, make it a point to introduce yourself to the concierge, which seals the deal.

- If the hotel has a swimming pool, tip the pool attendant (the amount you give will depend on the quality of the hotel, since there's a difference between a five-star hotel and a small beachside operation). But if there is an area around the pool you particularly want to sit in, or two especially plush-looking lounge chairs that you want, make your needs known, accompanied by a tip of approximately twenty dollars a day.

- When in doubt, I err on the side of offering a tip. In all my years of travel, I have never had anyone refuse the gratuity, with the exception of one or two top-position hotel managers. After all, the hospitality business is a service business! If someone refuses a tip you offer, realize that it may be a company policy he or she must follow, or a personal sense of responsibility to serve you without being paid. You might say, "Thank you. This has been a wonderful experience, and I look forward to recommending your establishment/business to all my friends." Referrals are, after all, one of the highest and most authentic compliments you can give.

Tipping in Restaurants

The Maître D'

In theory, the maître d' of a respectable restaurant will be far too professional to accept money for a good table. In reality, it is fairly common for a maître d' to accept cash. What's important is that you create a rapport with the maître d' of a restaurant you enjoy. Make a point of asking the maître d's name and getting his or her card before you leave, as well as saying something specific that might help him remember you, such as asking him about himself or sharing a sincere compliment about the experience you just had. If you plan to dine at the restaurant often, make it a point to thank him or her when you leave, and slip a gratuity into his or her hand as a thank-you.

The amount given depends upon the restaurant and can be loosely based on what's paid to the waiter or waitress as gratuity for their services. Since you won't be giving money to the maître d' each time you dine, tip him generously. The more generous the tip, the quicker you'll be seated. Thirty or forty dollars will get you a table immediately, a gesture I'll make approximately every two months if I dine at the establishment frequently. The important thing is to keep the relationship alive! If you find yourself seated at a back table, it may be a sign that your relationship needs watering!

When I call again to make a reservation, I ask the reservations person if I can speak with the maître d'. Usually, he or she will assume that I have an ongoing relationship and I'm given a good table. If I don't know the reservations person, I try to find a friend or someone who's familiar with the restaurant and willing to make the reservation on my behalf.

The Waiter

Reward excellent service accordingly: anywhere from 15 to 20 percent of your meal—net of sales tax. If the service has been less than ideal, you can leave a lesser percent of the bill or, if your waiter has been rude or inattentive, nothing. If the service is really shockingly awful, excuse yourself from the table and speak with the maître d' or manager on duty and ask for another server for the rest of the meal.

By no means should a diner be expected to honor the same percentages when it comes to very expensive bottles of wine or liquor. Tips are a diner's prerogative. They are up to the tipper—not the person who's being tipped. I tend to tip 20 percent of the food, then I add on at least 10 percent of the wine.

A Cash Advance

I will often pretip in a restaurant, particularly if I am hosting a large party of friends. I take the waitpersons aside beforehand and let them know that if they take good care of me, I will take good care of them. Nine times out of ten, my waiter or waitress will get the message! Often I will pass the waitpersons some cash right then and there, based on a rough estimation of what I know the meal will end up costing. When the final

Bad Service Turned Good

You've generously doled out tips to the concierge, the pool attendant, the trainer who runs the sports complex behind your hotel, the waiter or waitress in your hotel's four-star restaurant, but something goes wrong.

Here's what to do:

- Let the management know at once what's bothering you. Address the problem calmly immediately when it occurs and *not* after you have left the hotel. Often guests will suffer through a substandard stay and wait until they get home to write an unpleasant letter to the hotel management, claiming that their stay was compromised or even ruined. While it might feel good to get this off your chest in the privacy of your own home, it won't give you the satisfaction of resolving the problem in the first place. If you had complained right away, the hotel would have had the opportunity to remedy the situation and turn a negative into a positive.

- Phrase your complaint reasonably and specifically, without shouting or threatening. Let the general manager know that the service or the experience is inadequate, or not what you expected. "I was very much looking forward to my trip," you can say, "but here is what seems to be happening. What can you do to fix it?" The clearer you are about the problem, the easier it is for others to solve it to your satisfaction. Many problems are compounded because of poor communication.

Most hotel managers will make an honest, concerted effort to fix something that's gone wrong. The hospitality business aims to please and to put guests at their ease.

- Depending on the nature of your complaint, I advise formulating in your head a reasonable remedy for it. "What can we do to make up for the situation?" is among the first questions people trained in customer or guest relations are poised to ask. Whether you would like to change rooms or have something taken off your bill as consolation for the nauseating smell of wet paint, or even change hotels entirely, make it clear what the management can do to salvage your trip. But again, be reasonable. The more reasonable you are, the more the manager will want to help you.

- Back at home, decide whether or not the management handled your complaint properly. Depending on the quality of your experience there, inform your travel agent, if you use one, to recommend the hotel to his or her other clients, or to steer clear.

- If I've had a particularly good visit at a hotel, I take the time to write to the hotel manager on my personal stationery, saying something like "Thank you for making me feel so welcome during my recent stay, and here's wishing you a successful summer." Believe me when I say that these kinds of notes go a long way! Next year, when you are placing a reservation at the same hotel, the response will doubtlessly be similar to what I've received, "Hello, Mr. Cowie! Welcome back!"

bill arrives, I'll make the necessary calculations to ensure it comes out fair for everyone. If the service that evening was truly spectacular, I might leave more money on top of what I have already given my server up front, even if the restaurant has automatically added a gratuity to the bill. If the service was adequate, I'll leave the tip as is. If the service wasn't up to par, and it's necessary to revise the gratuity, do so on your invoice before signing the bill and not afterward. Credit card companies are hesitant to reverse charges for services received.

Tipping is yet one more unknown of traveling, but knowing the basics will help you navigate your way easily and confidently through any and all unfamiliar situations, whether it's a crowded airport, an unfamiliar hotel, or the hottest new restaurant down the block or in a faraway city. By anticipating the unavoidable elements of travel—predeparture stress, endless ticket lines, traffic jams, road construction, jet lag, smoky hotel rooms, mediocre food, or the amount to slip the pool attendant for that unbeatable place in the sun—you'll feel confident and ready to triumph wherever you land (with your sanity and equilibrium intact). Whether you're traveling by train or by car, taking a thirteen-hour plane trip to South Africa, or landing the choicest booth in your favorite restaurant, the more preparation you do in advance—and the more know-how you stow away in your suitcase—the better able you'll be to showcase your best possible self and to live your best possible life. The sky *is* the limit. Happy trails (and don't forget to breathe deeply)!

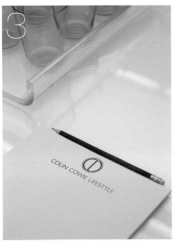

1 In my office as in my home, one of my virtues is order, since it paves the way for maximum creativity.

2 I keep my stationery in the drawer right next to me, so I can write thank-you notes first thing in the morning.

3 A fresh pad of paper and pencil await each visitor to our office.

4 A vibrant color scheme welcomes you into our New York offices.

1 I feel privileged to work with such talented people.

2 In this small conference room, I spend creative time, take meetings, and make presentations.

3 Order in the house!

4 Each desk has a fragrant candle and a carafe of water for an inspired working environment.

5—6 Our conference rooms are always set with beverages and snacks. A well-appointed one says "efficiency."

1 My pride and joy: my home office, just as it should be!

2 A vase of fresh flowers always inspires.

3 A shameless self-promoter, I always leave a copy of my latest book on my desk!

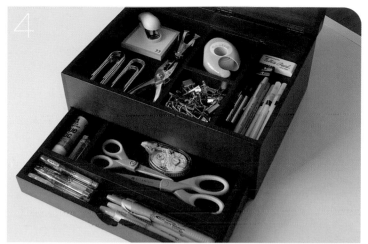

4 Within arm's reach of my desk is a compartmentalized wooden box filled with every conceivable office supply.

5 By all means, separate church and state when you work from your house or apartment, but don't deny yourself those little touches that make it feel like home.

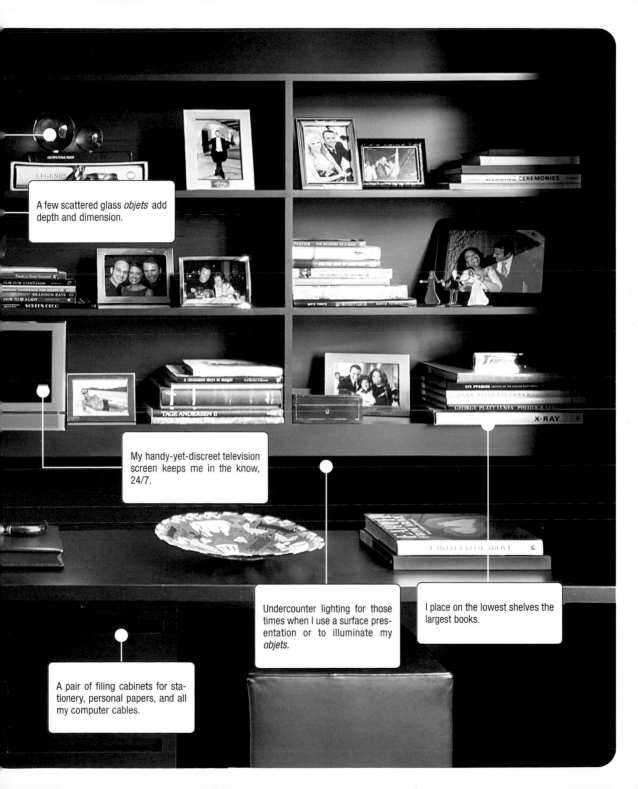

A few scattered glass *objets* add depth and dimension.

My handy-yet-discreet television screen keeps me in the know, 24/7.

Undercounter lighting for those times when I use a surface presentation or to illuminate my *objets*.

I place on the lowest shelves the largest books.

A pair of filing cabinets for stationery, personal papers, and all my computer cables.

A pile of paper used for recycling.

Rubber bands, glue sticks, and assorted office supplies.

Reusable plastic folders for inter-office.

My favorite toy, the labelmaker. (Everything in my life is labeled. It puts everything in the right spot.)

Ink cartridges, which we return to the computer store for recycling.

Packing supplies (tape, peanuts, bubble wrap) are kept handy in a large plastic container.

BATTERIES

POST-IT FLAGS

ERASERS

GLUE STICKS & WITE OUT

SMALL PAPER CLIPS

SMALL BINDER CLIPS

SCISSORS

SMALL POST-ITS

PENCILS

ULTRA FINE & FINE SHARPIES

MEDIUM PAPER CLIPS

MEDIUM BINDER CLIPS

STAPLES

MEDIUM POST-ITS

BLACK PENS

SHARPIES

LARGE PAPER CLIPS

STAPLER REMOVERS

LARGE POST-ITS

RED PENS

COLORED SHARPIES

RUBBER BANDS

COLORED LABELS

COLORED POST-ITS

PEN REFILLS

HIGHLIGHTERS

STAMPS

TAPE

brother PC-201

brother PC-201

PLASTIC FOLDERS

PACKING SUPPLIES

FedEx

FedEx

FedEx Ikox

FedEx Express

travel

gallery

1
Always place a towel on the bed before arranging your travel necessities. Who knows what's on the bottom of that suitcase that's been dragged in the trunk of a taxi for forty miles?

2
I keep all my cables, chargers, and electronic paraphernalia in clearly labeled cases.

3
Besides personal stationery, I always travel with small bills, for easy tipping.

4
I carry all my travel paperwork, including a detailed itinerary, in a reusable transparent plastic envelope.

1 Take a peek at the essentials of my carry-on luggage (which is either black or brown). I can get away with packing only a pair of dress shoes, a pair of exercise shoes, a few shirts, a pair of jeans, a pair of dress pants, and a maximum amount of accessories (e.g., sunglasses and belts, to change my look as often as the mood calls for). Add that to the pair of shoes and pants I wear on the plane, along with my carry-on sweater, and I'm good to go.

2 These plastic, transparent travel bags allow me to travel in the most orderly manner possible.

When you travel, surrender! *Everything* is out of your control. Your only concern should be to get to your destination safely and to bring enough reading material (and battery power) to deal with the ever-increasing delays we experience with today's travel.

I like to wear black when I travel. It's comfortable, casual, and always makes a great impression. I also tend to wear layers, cotton T-shirt, and a cashmere sweater on top of that.

Wearing techno-fabrics allow you to arrive on the other side without the creases of a turkey's neck.

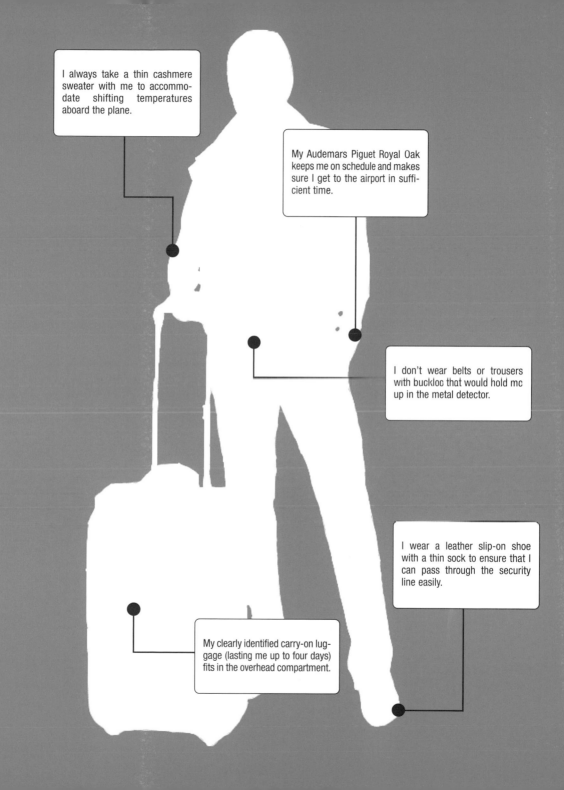

conclusion

Colin Cowie Chic has been a lifetime in the making. After all, each of us is born with the basic hardware but we need to have that all-important software installed. Over the years, it's been my privilege and pleasure to meet and work with some of the most extraordinary people in the world, and the lessons I've learned from them have helped me navigate through life, Aston Martin–fast, first class all the way! I hope I've now passed these lessons — this software — on to you.

I must admit, I lead the most charmed life imaginable. I get a lot of satisfaction in helping people dream up good times, usher in happiness, and create lasting memories! At the end of the day, there is no downside to my job. Still, as with any fulfilling work, it's not always a bed of roses (I could write a whole book on party catastrophes and how my team and I managed to avert disaster!). But all of the varied moments — from the sublime to the ridiculous — have shaped my journey and shown me that if style and elegance infuse everything you do, things tend to turn out rather well. Indeed, there are enormous rewards that come from living your best possible life . . . and I honestly believe that those who put in the most effort, who pay attention to every detail, who consider the people around them every step of the way — in short, those people who make a point of really showing up — are the ones who've found the *true* meaning of "success."

In many ways, *Colin Cowie Chic* is very much a sign of the times. We've graduated to a new way of living — and are freer than ever before to exercise our options, design our futures, and improvise our lives as we go along. And to support this new thinking, there have never been more services available to us, from Web sites to retailers, that radiate style and offer fantastic professional advice, twenty-four hours a day, seven days a week.

So fill your days and your home with family and friends. Dim the overhead bulbs. Light the candles. Mix the cocktails. It doesn't matter if the beef is medium instead of rare, or if the soufflé droops instead of rises. If my book has taught you nothing else, I hope you'll remember this: Life is not, and should never be, about doing things "perfectly." Your best is more than good enough, so long as you do it with über-amounts of generosity, humility, grace, passion, style, glamour, fabulousness . . . and of course fun!

Here's to living your life as it should be!

acknowledgments

This book has taken me a lifetime to live . . . and many years to assemble. Capturing my voice for this book has been no easy feat. I clearly don't do all this alone and have never been one to be shy with gratitude — so, first, a big thank-you to Lisa Kogan and Peter Smith for your passion and dedication in doing such an amazing writing job. Heartfelt thanks to my friends, my coworkers, and all the hosts and hostesses around the globe whom I've worked with, respect, and continue to learn from. Thanks to Colin Miller for capturing my life's passions by photographing the big pictures and the small details that really *do* make a difference. A huge debt of gratitude to the team at Clarkson Potter for believing in this project and bringing so much passion to the table: my editor, Aliza Fogelson; Marysarah Quinn in the art department; book designer Jennifer Beal; publisher Lauren Shakely; and editorial director Doris Cooper. I thank my business partner David Berke and my life and soul partner, Stuart Brownstein, for providing me with the support to move this exciting project forward. Living my best life possible requires a lot of slicing, dicing, ironing, and steaming — all courtesy of my housekeeper and "other mother," Gertrude Kleszczewski; she helps me to keep it moving at 120 miles per hour! And finally, to my parents, who instilled in me a passion for living and a lifelong understanding of what it means to truly live with style: Always be considerate of others!

acknowledgments

index

index

credits